OUR TEAM /

FOUNDER

Hugo Taylor Black

SUB EDITOR

Louise Baxter

DESIGN

Hugo Taylor Black

PHOTOGRAPHY

Provided by Venues
Amy Fraser
Andrew Worssam
Dominic Loneragan
Edward De Simone
Hellene Algie
Honeydieu Fitography
Hugo Taylor Black
Joel Pratley
Katherine Lu
Natalia Horinkova
Romy Frydman

WEBSITE

Empowered

CONTRIBUTIORS /

LIBBY BABET

Libby is an author, presenter and entrepreneur. She's a trainer for Channel Ten's *The Biggest Loser: Transformed,* fitness expert for *Women's Fitness Magazine* and the Hit Network.

SCOTT GOODING

Scott is an Australian chef, health coach, author and thought leader, encouraging and inspiring people to cook real food at home for themselves and their loved ones.

JACKIE ALEXANDER

Jackie is the co-founder and studio manager of immersive yoga studio, Humming Puppy. Since opening in Sydney in 2015, she has expanded to open studios in Melbourne and New York.

JONNI POLLARD

Jonni is an internationally recognised meditation and wisdom teacher who has dedicated his life to sharing ancient knowledge gained from some of the greatest living masters of our time.

ADIE ROBERTSON

Adie's vision as founder of To Wonderland is to bring wellness to the world through preventative health, detoxification, relaxation and nutrition. She loves to practice and teach Dru yoga & meditation.

CONTENTS /

FOREWORD /

I'm so grateful for the opportunity to write the foreword for *The Wellness Guide*. My personal mission is to help people find just a little more happiness in their everyday, to feel good and live life to the full.

ALL OF THE BUSINESSES IN THIS BOOK ARE DOING IMPORTANT WORK FOR THEIR COMMUNITIES TO HELP THEM DO JUST THAT.

To those businesses, I say thank you and keep up the great work, I know first-hand how tough running a business can be but the world needs you. Health and fitness is definitely one of the best paths to happiness and a life well lived.

To you, the reader, thank you for supporting this passion for the health and wellness message. Communities are nothing more than a collection of people, so anything that improves the individual also improves the whole. Healthier, happier people make for better communities, it's as simple as that. If we want to live in a better world, each of us needs to take responsibility to improve ourselves - and if you're reading this, chances are that's what you're doing.

Throughout this book you'll find delicious cafes, boutique fitness studios, chilled-out yoga spaces and more. I'd encourage you to visit them all, connect with people and find your tribe because you really are the average of the people you hang out with the most.

You'll also get to tap into conversations with experts in fitness, nutrition, mindfulness and motivation. If what they have to say resonates with you, please look them up online and tell them so. Taking a few minutes to say "that helped me" is the greatest gift you can give to someone who's passionate about helping others.

And on that note, a big thank you to Hugo for his passion and taking the time to create this one-stop guide to all the best health hubs in Sydney. It's not always easy to find that little hole-in-the-wall cafe that passionately sources local produce; or the gym owners taking the time to create really special and effective programming; or the yoga studios going above and beyond with messaging that can change your state, if not the direction of your life. I know that I, for one, am looking forward to working my way through this book!

Finally, please remember that your health is a continuing evolving journey, not a final destination. Every individual body is unique, and curiosity and new experiences are required to keep your body and mind thriving. I hope this book helps guide your travels and puts a smile on your face as you navigate your way through.

LIBBY BABET

Health & Fitness Specialist

[NIMBUS & CO - BONDI BEACH]

INTRODUCTION /

The Wellness Guide was born from a simple mission: to compile and present an inspiring collection of health and wellness spaces, to empower Sydneysiders to live better, happier and healthier lives.

SYDNEY'S FAST PACE, COMBINED WITH THE DRIVE TO BECOME OUR PERSONAL BEST, MEANS WE'RE SEEING A MAJOR SOCIETAL SHIFT TOWARDS HEALTHIER LIFESTYLE CHOICES. BUT RATHER THAN STRIVING FOR PERFECTION, SYDNEYSIDERS ARE ON A QUEST FOR A FULFILLING LIFE BALANCE.

We have scoured the city to bring you the best in food, fitness, body, mind and soul, all in one beautiful book, with the hope it'll light the way on your wellness journey, or to inspire a new one.

Ranging from conscious eating and meditation to high-intensity interval training and specialty health-food stores, *The Wellness Guide* covers all the essentials for creating a holistic lifestyle.

Our Food section celebrates the diversity, innovation and nutritious trends among Sydney eateries and providores. Whether you're seeking wholesome home-cooking, nutritious takeaway, fresh seasonal produce or flavourful fine-dining, there's something for you to explore. From acai bowls and Ayurvedic menus to raw sweets and zesty seafood, the city is a melting pot of choice.

Looking to get into great shape, improve your confidence and meet new people? Our comprehensive Fitness guide features a broad spectrum of studios and classes, including boxing and martial arts, Pilates and yoga, spin, gymnastics, bootcamp, circuit training, and a range of unique sessions you may have never even heard of.

If your focus is on the big three – Body, Mind & Soul – we've sourced the best locations that will soothe your being, from traditional treatments to the cutting-edge. Slow down for a much-needed timeout and try a floatation tank, salt bath or cryotherapy session, or relax with a classic treatment at a boutique spa.

Not just a city guide, *The Wellness Guide* also includes a range of fascinating, inspirational articles by industry experts, covering the benefits of practices such as meditation, yoga, personal training, mindful nutrition and physical conditioning. Learn from people who authentically embody their wellness philosophies.

We also feature conversations with vibrant thought leaders on topics such as self-love, mindfulness, preventative treatment and the importance of giving back to the community. They share the catalysts for their passionate paths as well as their tactics, routine and habits for creating a happy, fulfilling life.

Thank you to our contributors for their knowledge and generous insight, and thank you for reading this labour of love. We hope *The Wellness Guide* provides you with practical and aspirational information that will leave you ready to take on the city and become the best version of yourself.

[NIMBUS & CO - BONDI BEACH]

KEY TO ICONS /

Beach View 

Dairy-Free Alternatives 

Dog-Friendly 

Gluten-Free Options 

Lockers 

Outdoor Seating 

Refuel Bar 

Robes 

Showers 

Tea Station 

Toiletries 

Towels 

Vegetarian / Vegan Options 

Yoga Mats 

FOOD

HEALTHY RESTAURANTS & CAFES
VEGAN + VEGETARIAN. ACAI BOWLS
SALAD BARS. HEALTH FOOD STORES
SUPERFOOD BARS. WHOLEFOODS

ACRE EATERY

31A Mallett St, Camperdown

SERVING /

Breakfast
Lunch
Dinner
Organic
Free Range
Kombucha

LOYAL TO LOCAL • Acre Eatery is a farm-to-table restaurant, part of the revitalised community hub, Camperdown Commons. Their mission is to create consciousness around everyday food choices by providing a sustainable menu focused on transparency, seasonality and traceability. This starts with being 'loyal to local' by limiting food travel to no more than eight metres from the restaurant; prioritising sustainable produce from the on-site, four-season farm run by Pocket City Farms. Together with other small to medium sized local farms, Acre strives to highlight the abundance of New South Wales on the menu. You may have heard of 'nose to tail', but Acre also works with the approach of 'root to tip', ensuring all off-cuts from protein and produce are used to minimise waste and maximise yield. All proteins are sustainably sourced.

ACREEATERY.COM.AU

ALBERT & MOORE

Chatswood & Freshwater

SERVING /

Breakfast
Lunch
Cold Pressed Juices
Smoothies
Raw Treats

WARM WELCOME • Albert and Moore Cafe prides itself on being a true local eatery where everyone is welcomed and considered. At its two locations – the original in Freshwater and a second cafe in Chatswood – the philosophy is all about 'loving the food that loves you back'. With a menu offering fresh produce and diverse dietary options, there is a wholesome and nutritious meal for even the most discerning diner. The cafes cater for gluten free, paleo, vegetarians and vegans and specialises in breakfast and lunch. Think green goodness bowls, hearty brunches, tasty stacks, cold-pressed juices and single-origin coffee. Bright and airy interiors offer the warming touch of home, where you can take a seat and feel at ease. If you're in Freshwater, it could be the perfect pitstop before or after a beach visit – or perhaps both.

ALBERTANDMOORE.COM

BILLS

Bondi Beach, Darlinghurst & Surry Hills

SERVING /

Coffee
Breakfast
Lunch
Dinner
Dessert

LIVING LEGACY • Renowned restaurateur and food writer Bill Granger takes a relaxed approach to food, and his restaurants reflects this distinctly Australian spirit: sunny, easygoing and generous.
In 1993, at the age of 24, Bill dropped out of art school and opened his first restaurant in Darlinghurst. It soon became loved for its legendary breakfasts, served at the famous central communal table, where locals, travellers, families and friends continue to be welcomed. Twenty Five years later, Bill's approach has become truly global, and is enjoyed at his restaurants in Sydney - at Darlinghurst, Bondi Beach and Surry Hills - as well as Seoul, Tokyo, Honolulu and London. The enduring popularity of Bills can be attributed to good, fresh food, breezy service and an infectiously joyful atmosphere that is welcoming to everyone.

BILLS.COM.AU

THE BOATHOUSE SHELLY BEACH

1 Marine Pde, Manly

SERVING /

Coffee
Breakfast
Lunch
Cocktails
Seafood

BEACHSIDE BEAUTY • A light, bright and airy venue on the shores of Shelly Beach, The Boathouse is the epitome of seaside sophistication. The Boathouse Shelly Beach is a Manly favourite that offers modern-Australian menus for breakfast and lunch, with a focus on fresh, quality ingredients. Enjoy fresh flowers and water views from inside the cafe or in the outdoor courtyard, which is surrounded by tropical landscaped gardens. There's also a kiosk out the front that's perfect for a post-dip takeaway coffee or some fish and chips to eat on the beach. This picture-perfect cafe is fully licensed and available for weddings and events. It's part of The Boathouse Group established by Pip and Andrew Goldsmith in 2008, which has eight iconic waterside hospitality venues in Sydney.

THEBOATHOUSEGROUP.COM.AU

Breakfast

THE BOTANICA VAUCLUSE

2 Laguna St, Vaucluse

SERVING /

Breakfast
Lunch
Dinner
Farm-to-fork Produce

FEED THE SOUL • The Botanica Vaucluse is a relaxed food and retail destination in the heart of the eastern suburbs. Nestled among fragrant herbs, spices, citrus trees and berry bushes, it's a leafy oasis in a central location. The Botanica Vaucluse has a farm-to-fork philosophy that celebrates the seasons, with ethically and sustainably sourced produce from its Jamberoo Valley Farm and local suppliers, or freshly picked from the venue's kitchen garden. Open for lunch and dinner with breakfast available on weekends, the restaurant delivers sophisticated modern cuisine that lets the ingredients do the talking. There's also a range of delicious drinks available, including house-made gin, and natural, organic and biodynamic wines from varying Australian regions. If you feel so inclined, there's an on-site spa with a menu of nourishing signature treatments including facials, massages and acupressure.

THEBOTANICAVAUCLUSE.COM.AU

BREAD & CIRCUS

21 Fountain St, Alexandria

SERVING /

Breakfast
Lunch
Coffee
Cold Pressed Juices
Smoothies

A BRUNCH ABOVE • Booming with eclectic food stores and cafes, inner-city suburb Alexandria is a destination for innovation. One venue contributing to this wave is Bread and Circus Wholefoods Canteen – a breakfast and lunch specialist focused on organic and biodynamic dishes. As a 'wholefoods canteen', the food is produce-driven and lets the ingredients do the talking. Think of a fragrant breakfast curry, a seasonal fruit plate, unapologetically garlicky Nicola potato salad or dreamy pumpkin, sweet potato and chilli coconut soup. There's also a 'fine tea' menu and comprehensive drinks list to work your way through. From coffee classics, cold brew and filter varieties, to cold-pressed juices, hot chocolate, smoothies and kefir. The 'liquid lama' looks a treat – filtered coffee with grass-fed butter and organic virgin coconut oil. The rustic warehouse decor and communal tables create a welcoming vibe for relaxed dining.

BREADANDCIRCUS.COM.AU

BROTH BAR & LARDER

49 Belgrave St, Bronte

SERVING /

Bone Broth
Fermented Drinks
Lunch
Raw Treats
Soups

DRINK TO YOUR HEALTH • Broth Bar and Larder fuses old-world wisdom and traditions with a contemporary offering that champions health and longevity. This was Sydney's first dedicated broth bar, opened in 2015 by Soulla Chamberlain, the director of wholefoods brand Star Anise Organic Wholefoods. Soulla is a traditional foods cooking instructor, a health coach and a wellness blogger, and she's on a mission to bring nutrient-dense, whole, unprocessed foods back to the modern table. Broth Bar and Larder is a small and inviting space to enjoy homemade, nourishing foods, including bone broths, broth-based soups, a slow-cooked meal of the day, chicken liver pate, activated nuts, and guilt-free raw treats. All products are handcrafted in small batches on-site and are made from organic ingredients including 100% pastured meat.

CHISWICK

65 Ocean St, Woollahra

SERVING /

Lunch
Dinner
Fresh Garden Produce

CHARMING SIMPLICITY • Nestled in Sydney's picturesque Woollahra, Chiswick offers casual dining in a stunning setting. With many ingredients grown outside in the kitchen garden, the menu is alive to the seasons. Owned and operated by famed chef and restaurateur, Matt Moran, the Chiswick restaurants reflect the simplicity of produce-driven cooking. The approach is something altogether natural and continually evolving, where the emphasis is on where the food comes from and how it is grown. For example, the famous Chiswick lamb is sourced from the Moran family farm, located in the Central Tablelands of NSW. Filled with natural light, Chiswick contemporary dining room gives way to a casual bar area, large communal table and shaded outdoor seating – perfect for a quick bite or drink, a special celebration or Sunday lunch with the family.

CHISWICKWOOLLAHRA.COM.AU

CONCRETE JUNGLE

58 Kensington St, Chippendale

SERVING /

Coffee
Breakfast
Brunch
Cold Pressed Juices
Kombucha
Smoothies

CENTRAL OASIS • Located in the heart of Chippendale, Concrete Jungle is a serene oasis from the hustle of Sydney's busy streets. Using fresh local produce, the cafe aims to create dishes that make you feel good from the inside out. The plant-based menu is accompanied with ethically sourced meats to promote the benefits of sustainable eating. There's all-day breakfast with dishes including Bircher muesli, smashed avocado with coconut feta, and nourish bowls, and a lunch menu featuring roasted cauliflower salad and housemade gnocchi. The delicious plates and bowls of food are filled with vibrant ingredients that almost look too good to eat. Enjoy your meal or coffee in a contemporary, airy space, filled with greenery and natural light.

CONCRETEJUNGLECAFE.COM

COOH

90-96 Bourke Rd, Alexandria

SERVING /

Breakfast
Lunch
Dinner
Fresh Juices
Kombucha
Raw Treats
Smoothies

HONESTLY GOOD • Located in the industrial hot spot of Alexandria, COOH has a more nature-inspired, wholesome food philosophy: 'honest food, full of flavour.' Founded with this passionate mission, COOH provides a variety of well-rounded meals, vegan smoothies, farm-fresh juices and house-roasted coffee to the local community. They pride themselves on the use of fresh, local ingredients, to support like-minded small wholesalers and regional farmers. COOH is open both day and night. For breakfast, find favourites such as a vegan peanut-butter latte or gluten-free buckwheat pancakes with seasonal fruit and coconut yoghurt. Later, there's cumin-spiced cauliflower salad, fresh herbs, pine nuts and tahini for lunch, or crispy-skin Ora king salmon with sweet potato puree for dinner. The large, contemporary, light-filled space is a great place to relax and unwind with beautiful fare.

COOH.COM.AU

THE COOK ROOM

49-53 North Steyne, Manly

SERVING /

Dinner
Kombucha
Kombucha Cocktails
Kids Menu

FEEL-GOOD MEALS • The Cook Room was born out of the desire to provide a natural and nourishing dinner for the community; a place where you can gather with family, friends and neighbours in a beautiful beachfront setting. Driven by the passion and mission to create food with natural ingredients, handmade from scratch each day, the restaurant delivers the kind of meal that makes you feel good afterwards. All ingredients are organic, from the 'clean 15 list' and with no added preservatives or hormones. The warm and inviting restaurant welcomes vegans, vegetarians, meat-eaters and diners intolerant to gluten and dairy. Try a selection share plates or a larger main for yourself, then maybe enjoy one of their signature desserts. Drinks wise, there's a selection of great Australian wines, beers and ciders and housemade kombucha.

THECOOKROOMMANLY.COM

EGG OF THE UNIVERSE

711 Darling St, Rozelle

SERVING /

Breakfast
Lunch
Fresh Juices
Kombucha
Raw Treats
Smoothies

MADE WITH LOVE • Sydney's only integrated yoga studio and wholefoods cafe, 'The Egg' provides delicious, nourishing food to complement the mindful yoga practice offered in the studio. The menu is a fun and modern exploration of the wholefoods concept, ruled by taste, led by the seasons and inspired by traditional wisdom. All core ingredients are sourced from high-quality producers and providores, in line with the principles of sustainable, organic farming. Whether you seek to celebrate with coffee and cake, cleanse with green smoothies and broth or delve into deep nourishment with slow-cooked stews, there's something to satisfy. The delightful urban garden setting is open seven days and is a perfect place to unwind after a yoga session – whether enjoying a fresh, hearty breakfast or a coffee, juice or signature drink such as the roasted dandelion latte.

EGGOFTHEUNIVERSE.COM

GIRDLERS

Brookvale, Dee Why Beach & Manly

SERVING /

Breakfast
Brunch
Lunch
Fresh Juices
Kombucha
Organic Coffee
Raw Treats
Smoothies

SIMPLE AND HONEST • After retiring from professional football, Ryan Girdler developed a new passion: specialty coffee and roasting. The Girdlers cafe journey began in 2005 when Ryan and his partner Katja took over a small cafe on Dee Why Beach. Sebastian, their Colombian partner, joined a few years later and the trio set about creating a health-conscious, community-oriented food emporium on Sydney's Northern Beaches. A place where people from all walks of life can mingle and enjoy their shared passion for natural, tasty foods. There are now three Girdlers cafes in the region. With beautifully designed boho interiors and wholesome food, the venues champion a lifestyle of wellness, with a commitment to using local suppliers, honest ingredients and sustainable practices. From athletes to vegans and children with food sensitivities, Girdlers strives to cater for everyone.

GIRDLERS.COM.AU

GIRDLERS

HEART CAFE

95 Roscoe St, Bondi Beach

SERVING /

Breakfast
Lunch
Cold Pressed Juices
Probiotic Drinks
Smoothies

HEARTFELT HOSPITALITY • If you love community, Heart Cafe is a great place to meet up, relax and enjoy beautiful fresh food and coffee, served with love – right in the heart of Bondi. As Bondi's first social enterprise cafe, the Heart Cafe helps to return hope to the lives of disadvantaged young people by supporting them in paid hospitality traineeships for 12 months. They are able to give back to the local community by providing gourmet breakfasts, healthy salad bowls and bespoke dishes. The Heart Cafe also follows a local and sustainable food philosophy with a delicious wholefood menu using fresh, local ingredients, including organic produce sourced directly from the Wayside Chapel Community Garden, less than 50m away. There are gluten-free, vegetarian, vegan and dairy-free alternatives, as well as food options and activities for kids in a family-friendly atmosphere.

LITTLE JEAN

1 Kiaora Rd, Double Bay

SERVING /

Breakfast
Lunch
Dinner
Wine
Cocktails

DAY TO NIGHT • Little Jean is a bistro that offers a daily menu of fresh, seasonal and local produce, with a focus on sustainable and ethical suppliers. The light-filled interior is minimalistic and breezy with two distinct zones: a dining space and a casual area with a communal table, bar or window seating stools. Takeaway orders are also available from there. For a great start to the day, head in for some house-made pastries, great coffee, down-to-earth service and a calming space to enjoy your breakfast or maybe head in for lunch to treat yourself. Little Jean is not just a daytime venue. At night, it transforms into a relaxed diner with friendly service, beautifully presented fresh food and great local wines, with some of Australia's best on the menu.

LOX STOCK AND BARREL

140 Glenayr Ave, Bondi Beach

SERVING /

Breakfast
Lunch
Dinner
Baked Goods
Fermented Drinks
Smoothies

DOWN-TO-EARTH DELICACIES • Lox Stock and Barrel is a cosy, 40-seat deli diner in one of the last remaining old pockets of Bondi Beach. It's a modern interpretation of the classic delicatessen, which means "delicious food", and delivers food without pretension, that is simple to prepare and cooked from the heart, using what's fresh, abundant and in season. Lox Stock and Barrel's food is Jewish in origin, influenced by the best loved dishes of the owners' ancestors from pre-war Europe. But the offering is based on the best of local, seasonal produce and satisfying, balanced eating.
Enjoy a nourishing, flavourful, hearty meals for breakfast, lunch or dinner, and even cocktails in the eve. The kitchen is run as close to 'farm to plate' as possible, with the philosophy that cooking doesn't start with a recipe, it starts with great ingredients.

THE MEWS

3-5 Myahgah Rd, Mosman

SERVING /

Coffee
Breakfast
Lunch
Cold Pressed Juices
Smoothies

FEAST FOR THE SENSES • Set in the heart of Mosman Square, in a cosy, bustling alleyway, The Mews is a local gem with a loyal following. The healthy menu is inspired by a fusion of influences, from authentic Asian cuisine to modern Australian flavours. They pride themselves on serving stunning creations with immaculate details that excite the senses. Every element of each dish is well considered, from flavour combinations to the plating and final presentation, using hand-picked ingredients from the Flemington Markets. The breakfast and lunch menu offers a selection of classics with more innovative pairings, all based around fresh produce and tastes. There's a range of signature salads and vegan-friendly options available, too. Drinks wise, there's a diverse range of tea, juices, dairy-free smoothies and, of course, coffee. The Mews is also a licensed venue.

THEMEWSMOSMAN.COM.AU

THE NINE

163 Glenayr Av, Bondi Beach

SERVING /

Coffee
Breakfast
Lunch
Dinner

GOOD TASTE • Nestled in the heart of Bondi Beach, The Nine is a sustainable cafe that incorporates nine core Mediterranean cuisines into its seasonal farm-to-table menu, using the best-quality organic and chemical-free ingredients. Signature all-day dishes include the Turkish baked eggs, haloumi croquettes, Persian avo smash and rustic mushrooms on toast. Wellness porridge or a coyo chia bowl provide a tasty morning boost. The beverages list includes natural and biodynamic wines and progressive organic cocktails, fresh probiotic juices and luxury teas. The Nine has carved a loyal customer base for distinctive focus and philosophies, showcasing the Mediterranean diet and Bondi lifestyle with an ethical and community-based approach. Housed in a vibrant seaside space, designed by one of Sydney's top architects, the cafe captures the casual, quintessentially Sydney style, with premium menu options.

THENINESYDNEY.COM.AU

ORA

17B Whistler St, Manly

SERVING /

Breakfast
Lunch
Beet Kvass
Fresh Juices
Kombucha
Raw Treats
Smoothies

IN-HOUSE HEALTH • Set in a peaceful space in Manly, Ora was created for people to nourish their bodies and calm their minds. It's a place where you don't need to worry about what's in your meal or how it's cooked – everything is prepared properly with organic ingredients that are ethically grown and raised alongside environmental considerations. Everything is prepared and cooked in-house (except for the sourdough and full-cream milk) and is made with a purpose. In Maori, ora means 'to survive, be alive, well, safe, cured, fit, recovered, healthy, healed' – a message that's on their wall and informs everything they do. The Ora team advises you to be open-minded to what they have to offer: they will cook for you as they would cook for their family, based on the mission to provide goodness, health and happiness for everyone.

ORAMANLY.COM.AU

ORCHARD STREET

2 Brighton Blvd, North Bondi

SERVING /

Breakfast
Lunch
Organic Coffee
Kombucha

NATURAL REMEDIES • Channeling the ancient and modern arts of healing into life-enhancing offerings, Orchard Street is dedicated to 'true wellness'. The Elixir Bar in North Bondi sits on a peaceful and sunny corner, not far from the beach. Hot herbal elixirs, organic coffee, kombucha on tap and a delicious range of nourishing delights are available to eat in or takeaway. Find support, guidance and inspiration to enhance your health, with Orchard Street's collective of natural health practitioners at the North Bondi Clinic. Orchard Street was founded in early 2013 by Kirsten Harvey, a qualified naturopath, herbalist and nutritionist with the mission to elevate the collective experience of wellness. Each product has been expertly created to conjure a positively thriving state of body, mind and spirit; a 'way of being' aligned with the wisdom of nature.

 ORCHARDSTREET.COM.AU

OUROBOROS

118 Devonshire St, Surry Hills

SERVING /

Breakfast
Lunch
Cold Pressed Juices
Smoothies
Raw Treats

FROM THE INSIDE OUT • Ouroboros is a light-filled wholefoods cafe in Surry Hills, based on the philosophy 'you are what you eat'. To illustrate this, the centrepiece is an expansive mural of the ancient ouroboros symbol: a serpent eating its own tail. Make the most of the all-day breakfast menu and sink your teeth into dishes such as the flavoursome zucchini and corn fritters. The lunch menu is colourful and wholesome with Buddha bowls, fresh salads and an array of cold-pressed juices made on site. The space is light and bright with large, wooden, communal tables and winding ivy, making it ideal for big groups. So whether you're looking to grab a coffee, quench your thirst with a kombucha (or a cheeky pinot grigio) or relieve those sugar cravings with a raw, sugar-free treat, Ouroboros will take care of you.

OUROBOROSCAFE.COM.AU

PORCH & PARLOUR

110 Ramsgate Ave, North Bondi

SERVING /

Breakfast
Lunch
Dinner
Fresh Juices
Smoothies

SEASIDE SOPHISTICATION • Whether you are rolling off the beach with the sand between your toes, on your way to work or settling in for dinner, Porch and Parlour has you covered. The dining experience is conducive to both sophisticated and casual dining, with great food, beverages and friendly, informed service, from breakfast through to dinner. The food is clean and simple yet progressive. Think breakfast bowls, house-made sprouted breads and spicy chai in the morning, or Cone Bay barramundi or a steak sandwich for lunch.

At night, the menu is share style with dishes such as freshly shucked Coffin Bay oysters, and Zanzibar beef skewers with charred pineapple relish. The wine list has 12 selections from mostly boutique Australian vineyards, and a rotating list of four biodynamic, organic, natural or sustainable wines by the glass.

PREACH CAFE

112 Campbell Pde, Bondi Beach

SERVING /

Breakfast
Lunch
Coffee
Cold Pressed Juices
Smoothies

DIVINE BY DESIGN • A quote carved in metal, hanging above a communal bar inside Preach Cafe, tells you what you need to know about their food philosophy: "to eat is human; to eat well is divine." This wholefoods eatery on Bondi's foreshore is serving up some pretty divine options, indeed: from 'pokecado toast' – avocado with chunks of salmon sashimi, edamame and other fresh ingredients – to protein shakes, cold-pressed juices and coffee, there's plenty of choice with plenty of flavour. Breakfast and brunch is served up all day, making it an ideal spot for a leisurely catch-up near the beach. The dishes are colourful, exciting, Insta-worthy treats that'll satisfy your sense (and stomachs). The interior design was completed by De Simone Design and combines a clean, minimalist design with raw materials and a fresh coastal colour palette.

DESIGN BY DE SIMONE DESIGN

PURE WHOLEFOODS

5/10 Darley Rd, Manly

SERVING /

Breakfast
Lunch
Smoothies
Cold Pressed Juices
Raw Treats
Kombucha

PURE LIFE FORCE • Pure Wholefoods is a blend of passion, quality food, a vibrant atmosphere and attention to detail, based in the heart of Manly. Established by two Paleo practitioners, it's become popular with those seeking out nutritious fare or paleo-friendly options, as well as vegan and vegetarian items. With the belief that organic and biodynamic food is full of 'pure life force', Pure Wholefoods meticulously selects certified organic fruit and vegetables to provide a healthy haven for foodies. Serving breakfast, lunch, coffee and drinks, Pure Wholefoods is a great place to pop into throughout the day, whether for a post-swim meal, a nourishing lunch, or a leisurely latte in a friendly space. If you want a caffeine-free fix, there's a range of alternatives including turmeric, matcha or dandelion lattes.

PUREWHOLEFOODS.COM.AU

ROUGH & BARE

Mona Vale & St Leonards

SERVING /

Breakfast
Lunch
Kombucha
Raw Treats
Smoothies

HEALTHY HIDEAWAY • Rough and Bare is a hidden-gem wholefoods cafe in Mona Vale, tucked away down a back street with plenty to see inside. It's a destination for you to relax with friends and be nourished from the inside out, offering friendly faces, unique drink options and food the way nature intended. The space has been described as 'fresh and inviting', with simple decor that lets the food and drinks take centre stage. Retreat into one of their intimate tables for a low-key brekkie with a loved one, or connect with others at a large communal table over a hot cup of' brothee' (bone broth). With a chilled ambience, welcoming vibe and food crafted with love, Rough and Bare is a cafe worth finding and exploring in your own time.

ROUGHANDBARE.COM.AU

RUBY LANE

200 Pittwater Rd, Manly

SERVING /

Breakfast
Lunch
Cold Pressed Juices
Kombucha
Organic Grocer
Raw Treats
Smoothies

HAPPY EATING • Driven by the mission to make health foods fun, social and inspirational, Ruby Lane focuses on wholesome, local food and hospitality. You'll eat yourself happy with dishes created from natural, seasonal and nutrient-dense ingredients. Think vibrant smoothies, organic coffee, nourishing bowls for breakfast or lunch, and organic wine with sticky braised beef ribs for special monthly dinners. The unfussy kids' menu features favourites without the added sugar, and the sweets cabinet is free of gluten and refined sugar. Meat is organic and pasture-raised and fish is sustainably caught. There's solar on the roof, an efficient recycling system, and food waste is turned into bio-energy. Ruby Lane also donates to The Sealife trust to help preserve and protect the turtles of the Northern Beaches. There's also monthly wellness workshops for a healthy dose of education.

RUBYLANE.COM.AU

SEA SALT SOCIETY

2-8 Darley Rd, Manly

SERVING /

Brunch
Lunch
Dinner
Organic Wines

SOUL FOOD • As the name suggests, Sea Salt Society is based near the beach and has the same breezy, nourishing approach to life inside. They know how important clean food is for the mind, body and soul, so all ingredients are carefully selected from local suppliers to make sure its nutrient-dense and freshly prepared every day. The extensive brekkie menu is served until 3pm, featuring hearty options like the Big Brekkie Toolkit or wholefood pancakes, to lighter fare such as the Rainbow Bowl with seasonal fresh fruit, or the zesty coconut Breakfast Panna Cotta. Dietary requirements are well catered for, including paleo, keto, vegan, vegetarian, dairy-free and gluten-free.
Whether you're after a quick post-surf coffee, a lazy brunch before hitting the sand, or dinner and a few cheeky cocktails with friends, you'll find an inviting spot to relax and enjoy great hospitality.

SEASALTSOCIETY.COM.AU

WARREN & HOLT

415-421 Illawarra Rd, Marrickville

SERVING /

Breakfast
Brunch
Cold Pressed Juices
Kombucha
Organic Elixirs
Smoothies

HEALING WITH HEART • Warren and Holt is the passion project of husband and wife team Mat and Sophie Budzevski, born from an 'aha' moment after a serious health scare. They've worked closely with head chef Nik Jovicki and registered nutritionist Steph Wearne to create a memorable food experience. Their aim is to share the health and environmental benefits of choosing locally and ethically sourced produce, presented as close as possible to its whole state without compromising on taste. Open for breakfast, brunch and lunch seven days a week, Warren and Holt offers flexible food choices suitable for those with allergies or preferring a gluten-free, vegan or dairy-free diet, or anything in between. Almost everything on the menu can be modified. It's all about creating an inclusive, delicious and nutritious food journey with transparency at its heart.

WARRENANDHOLT.COM.AU

ZUSHI

33 Barangaroo Ave, Barangaroo

SERVING /

Japanese Cuisine
Lunch
Dinner
Cocktails
Sake
Umeshu

SHARING IS CARING • The Zushi philosophy is simple: to create a no-fuss, value-for-money Japanese dining experience in Sydney where quality is priority. Part of that is celebrating what food means to people. Zushi specialises in coupling the subtlety and beauty of Japanese food with a modern twist, using carefully sourced local ingredients. Their dishes are designed to share, inspired by the love of sharing food with friends and family. Their commitment to Japanese cuisine is to honour the high-quality produce by creating visually arresting dishes and share their same love for food. Every customer is treated like they are walking into a welcoming home kitchen by making every dish *oishii* ('delicious'). So, ready your chopsticks and bring your appetite. From traditional bento boxes and tempura to innovative sashimi tacos, there's something to tempt all taste buds (and 90% of the menu is gluten-free).

ZUSHI.COM.AU

SUPAGAS

A MELTING POT /

Sydney's culinary diversity is one of its best qualities, one we should all get out and try. If you're committed to a certain way of eating, never fear – the demand for healthy food options means we're now spoilt for choice.

FOR THE LAST 10 YEARS, I'VE BEEN SPRUIKING THE MESSAGE THAT AUSTRALIANS NEED TO BE THE CUSTODIANS OF THEIR OWN HEALTH – STARTING BY CONSISTENTLY COOKING AT HOME WITH REAL FOOD AND LOVE.

However, in our busy, fast-paced society, it's just not practical or realistic to think that every sip, slurp, bite and crunch will be of something homemade.

So, when the desire or need to eat out arises, Sydney has some great choices – regardless of your budget – that also tick the health box. This city is a global hub, from which new trends emerge. In many ways Sydney is a thought leader and driver of health – Bondi Beach has the highest uptake of exercise per capita than anywhere in the world, so it stands to reason that dining choices cater to fitness-loving folks.

The movement in recent years, particularly in the cafe space, is towards plating up simple, good and honest food. More and more places are paying homage to local growers, farmers and producers and, of course, seasonal produce. Cafe owners are thinking and acting more local than they were perhaps five or ten years ago – which has influenced patrons to shift their thinking, too.

It's fair to say that areas such as Bondi and Manly are where cafes predominantly embrace trending health items and weave them into menus. They're not afraid to be innovative, hearing about new food discoveries from social media, patrons, podcasts and blogs and integrating these ideas.

This is the world we live in now; so much information is shared – some good, some bad – but the credible health information will eventually rise to the top and healthy hubs grab the ball and start running. New ingredients may raise some eyebrows and questions but they often soon become part of the Australian vernacular.

Sydney's multicultural diversity creates a smorgasbord of meals to try and enjoy. Before I arrived here 20 years ago, I hadn't experienced many of the flavours that fill our culinary hubs. Food is the cohesive gel of a city and Sydney has variety in spades. There are healthy options to be found in all types of cuisines, whether it be Lebanese, Indian or Greek – sometimes it requires you to be a little selective but there are few menus that are off the radar. Culinary choice is one of Sydney's most alluring qualities and I strongly recommend getting out and experiencing it. Take a trip to Fairfield, Parramatta, Marrickville, Bondi, Cabramatta or Haberfield and excite the palate with different cuisines.

There will always be the outlets that don't prescribe to 'real', whole food or locally sourced produce but the popularity of places that do is on the rise – and that's positive for everyone. Sydneysiders are wanting to experience good, honest and healthy food... and cultivating demand for it.

MY TOP 5 HEALTHY CAFES IN SYDNEY

1. The Good Place - *Miranda*
2. Chiswick - *Woollahra*
3. Macelleria - *Newtown & Bondi Beach*
4. Nahlini's - *Bondi*
5. Bread and Circus - *Alexandria*

HAPPY EATING!

SCOTT GOODING / *Scott is an Australian chef, health coach, author and thought leader – encouraging and inspiring people to cook real food at home for themselves and their loved ones. Scott breaks down the barriers to cooking healthy food with his simple, affordable, nourishing recipes.*

RECONDITIONED.ME | SCOTTGOODINGPROJECT.COM

ALIBI

6 Cowper Wharf Rd, Woolloomooloo

SERVING /

100% Plant Based
Dinner
High Tea
Cocktails
Snacks

HARBOURSIDE HIDEAWAY • Who said cocktail hour couldn't be healthy? Alibi is a destination cocktail bar at Woolloomooloo Wharf, offering a 100% plant-based dining menu for those who embrace wellbeing and want a unique option to indulge. Alibi is spearheaded by renowned US plant-based chef and restaurateur, Matthew Kenney, who designed a menu of small and large plates of clean ingredients that pack a flavour punch. Each dish is beautifully presented, ensuring all senses are satisfied. The sophisticated contemporary venue features lounge and bar seating, plus share tables. Signature bespoke cocktails are expertly mixed, shaken and stirred, inspired by local and international flavours. Alibi serves up modern classics and old favourites with a twist. There's also a curated wine list if that's more your style.

GATHERED KITCHEN

99 Glebe Point Rd, Glebe

SERVING /

100% Plant Based
Baked and Raw Rreats
Breakfast
Lunch
Fresh Juices
Organic Kombucha
Smoothies

MAKE & BAKE • Owners Pim Tummasombut and Matt McLennan opened Gathered Kitchen in August 2017 as a 100% plant-based cafe & bakery promoting animal-free food with an organic and wholefoods focus. The playful menu combines wholefood recipes with delicious vegan flavours and organic and gluten free ingredients covering sweet and savoury dishes. They make and bake on the premises, with the vegan artisan bakehouse serving up organic and refined sugar-free goods including their signature croissants, pain au chocolat, activated-charcoal cruffins, whole-fruit Danishes and pumpkin cinnamon scrolls. Gathered Kitchen has delightful window seating overlooking the street, plus a bright mezzanine and garden courtyard for sunny vibes.

 GATHEREDKITCHEN.COM.AU

NALINIS

1/1 Newland St, Bondi Junction

SERVING /

Indian Cusine
Coffee
Breakfast
Lunch
Dinner

HEALING INGREDIENTS • Nalini's is the first restaurant in Sydney to serve a fully probiotic-themed and 100% gluten-free menu, which underlies their philosophy to make wholesome, healthy, delicious foods that nourish the body. Drawing on Ayurvedic principles and traditional Indian flavours, the food and drink offering is steeped in ancient wisdom with the freshness of modern cooking. Signature dishes include dosa wraps – with filling options such as Indian falafel, masala potatoes, greens or roasted sweet potato – naked bowls, and an Ayurvedic thali, which features all six tastes in one meal: sweet, sour, salty, bitter, pungent and astringent. If you're looking for something light or sweet, try an Ayurvedic turmeric latte, a hot cacao, masala chai, coconut yoghurt lassi, ice-cream or mousse. There are also breakfast options, including warming porridge, and probiotic smoothies.

NALINIS.COM.AU

PAPERBARK

18 Danks St, Waterloo

SERVING /

Native Produce
Dinner
Cocktails
Minimum Intervention-Wine

ADVANCED AUSTRALIA FARE • Paperbark is the latest collaboration from the teams behind Verd Sydney, Joe's Sandwich Bar and the iconic Alfie's Kitchen, taking plant-based dining to the next level. Executive chef Joey Astorga has worked at some of Sydney's top fine-dining restaurants and has developed a menu that highlight some of the powerful flavours from native-Australian plants, like the smoke from cooking with paperbark. It also offers original creations such as hazelnut pate with roasted beetroot, salted plum and toasted wattle seed, and paperbark-smoked leek with kipfler potato and finger lime. For dessert, there's rhubarb and lemon myrtle mousse with strawberry and eucalyptus sorbet or miso roasted banana with chocolate and peanut butter mousse. Paperbark also showcases excellent Australian natural wines and botanical-infused spirits.

PAPERBARKRESTAURANT.COM

SEFA KITCHEN

292 Bondi Rd, Bondi

SERVING /

Dinner
Fresh Garden Produce
Vegetarian
Healthy Meze
Kombucha
Sustainable Wine

HONEST HOSPITALITY • Sefa means 'leisurely abundance" in most Middle Eastern languages and that informs the approach to Sefa Kitchen's food and hospitality. The restaurant is a Bondi institution, taking its diners to a bohemian corner of the Middle East in a hip strip on the lower slopes of Bondi Road. The ancient-inspired yet progressive menu is driven by local and seasonal produce, with a focus on quality, sustainability and sharing. The raised garden beds and herb walls in Sefa's quaint backyard provide living touches in meze plates and themed cocktails, served by the owner on plates he made himself. Sefa Kitchen's intimate 50-seater room is warm and sophisticated, making it perfect for dates or group gatherings. It's open for dinners seven days a week, but it fills up quickly so bookings are highly recommended.

SEFAKITCHEN.COM

SHIFT EATERY

241 Commonwealth St, Surry Hills

SERVING /

Breakfast
Lunch
Smoothies
Cold Pressed Juices
Raw Treats
Kombucha

MAKING THE SHIFT • At Shift Eatery, they believe veganism is the way of the future for the health of people and the planet and the welfare of animals. So their mission is to make eating vegan as simple and tasty as possible. From hearty sandwiches, delicious nourishing bowls and specialty coffee, to superfood lattes, vegan deli meats, cheeses and plant-based protein, the menu has been designed as an all-in-one resource for people making the shift to a vegan diet (and perhaps a vegan lifestyle). Once you've sampled the menu and experienced what's possible with plant-based food, you can buy some supplies from the deli to take home. All deli items are hand-picked and professionally taste-tested to ensure you've got the best possible tools (and treats) to make your transition to a different way of eating.

SHIFTEATERY.COM.AU

JOSH PORTEOUS /

Josh Porteous was born and bred in Sydney and did a Masters in International Business before working in the corporate management world for 12 years. In 2012, he left to volunteer across Asia and Africa in some of the poorest countries on earth. During this time, he founded The International Brothers and Sisters House and is now dedicated to helping others through his charity. His cafes, Bare Naked Bowls, support the cause.

TELL US ABOUT YOUR LIFE JOURNEY AND HOW THIS INSPIRED BARE NAKED BOWLS.

I met my wife in Tanzania, we were both placed in the same volunteer house together and it was love at first sight. We travelled around developing countries establishing our charity for the next 18 months, spending the majority of our time in Cambodia and Nepal. During this time, as you can expect, we experienced some ill health and had to have some time back in my wife's hometown of Santa Barbara to get better.

While there, Ashley introduced me to acai bowls, something she had been eating for years but I had never tried. I fell in love and it ultimately assisted us both getting back to good health and made us look more closely at what we were putting into our bodies. We moved back to Nepal but fell pregnant shortly after and decided to have our baby in Sydney, my hometown. At this stage, I had been away for almost three years living in developing countries and growing our charity, The International Brothers and Sisters House. We had no money coming in so we started playing around with some acai bowl recipes. After about six months, we knew we were onto something and so we made the big decision to spend all of our savings and launch Bare Naked Bowls in Manly. The rest, as they say, is history.

WHAT DRIVES YOUR DESIRE TO CONTRIBUTE TO THE WORLD?

I spent the majority of my post-school life in the corporate world; 12 years at Coca-Cola Amatil. It was a great time, I earnt a lot of money, I continued my education and climbed the corporate ladder and I was good at it. However, some holes started to appear and I wasn't happy. So, on a whim, I booked a trip to Cambodia to do some volunteering at an HIV orphanage just outside of Phnom Penh. It was during these two weeks that my whole life changed – for the first time ever, I was surrounded by people that cared for others and were not looking out for themselves as number one. I decided about halfway through to quit my job and spend a couple of years in developing countries to deeply understand the people, the communities and their needs.

Since 2013 I have met some incredible young men and women across a number of countries who have come from horrific abusive and brutal environments but are the most caring children and young adults I have ever met – a lot of them wanted to study further, so I decided to launch my charity and support them. I count myself extremely lucky being born and bred in a place like Manly, surrounded by beauty and all the luxuries of the first world. I believe it is my duty to help those less fortunate. It's the children that drive me to contribute and the impact I can have on their lives and the surrounding communities

WHAT WAS IT LIKE TO START BARE NAKED BOWLS?

It was frightening, I'd never done small business and I had never worked in a cafe. Luckily, small business isn't that different to big business and my wife is a master in the cafe. We put every last cent we had into opening up Bare Naked Bowls Manly and our first daughter, Indie, arrived two months before opening. It was an intense time. Then, after six months our little cafe exploded, which brought on bigger challenges. But they were all good problems to have.

WHAT ARE YOUR PREDICTIONS FOR THE FUTURE OF HEALTH & WELLNESS?

I believe we have seen a huge shift in what consumers want and it's a shift that needed to happen. Customers are demanding more for their dollar and they want it packed full of health benefits. Personally, I would like to see junk food priced out of the market so we can stop the affordability and convenience trends in that market, but I am not sure that is never going to happen. People need to further educate themselves on what good looks like in regards to what they put into their bodies because food does have a huge effect on who you are.

TACTICS, ROUTINES AND HABITS /

WHAT IS THE BEST OR MOST WORTHWHILE INVESTMENT YOU'VE EVER MADE?

That's an easy one for me: the investment I spent with my time to travel to Cambodia and have my first volunteering experience. This broke me free from the corporate grind and allowed me to create a life that I wanted, not one that was prescribed for me.

WHAT NEW BELIEF, BEHAVIOUR OR HABIT HAS MOST IMPROVED YOUR LIFE?

I would say getting into a fitness routine. From time to time I have lower back problems so I manage this by staying active – my physio-turned-trainer has developed a daily fitness schedule for me to strengthen my back and core. For anywhere between 30 and 90 minutes each day, I am either in the pool, in the gym, on my bike or doing running drills. My fitness, strength and clarity have all improved because of this.

WHAT IS YOUR BEST TIP FOR FEELING GOOD?

Understand what you are putting into your body, eat clean and fresh, and most importantly, stay active.

BANANA BLOSSOM

Bondi Beach, Bondi Junction, Brookvale, Manly & Mona Vale

SERVING /

Asian Salads
Lunch
Rice Paper Rolls
Kombucha
Organic Ice Tea

GOOD FOOD TO-GO • Banana Blossom Asian Salads has become something of a household name on Sydney's Northern Beaches, combining authentic Asian flavours with fresh local ingredients to create a healthy 'fast food' option. Husband and wife team, Nat and Ben Thomas, are no strangers to Asian cooking. Nat was born and raised in Thailand before moving to Australia in 1994, while Ben has dedicated 15 years to mastering the cuisine. Banana Blossom has evolved organically since opening in 2003. Following their initial success, the pair opened an Asian deli in Mona Vale in 2007, selling traditional food and three special salads – this became a salad-only eatery in 2009, with 14 delicious options to-go.

FISHBOWL

Over 11 Restaurants in Sydney

SERVING /

Lunch
Dinner
Japanese Salads
Local Kombucha

SUPER BOWLS • Following a trip to California, where a new wave of salad bars was emerging, Nathan Dalah, Nic Pestalozzi and Casper Ettelson decided to combine their love of fine food with casual, quick and accessible service. The result was Fishbowl, which opened in Bondi in the summer of 2016. The friends wanted to make the most of Australia's access to high-quality seafood and produce with a destination that offered beautiful, healthy Japanese salads made fresh to order. Fishbowl provides premium, sustainable ingredients, with a particular penchant for sashimi, so you can build your own bowl from base to toppings or choose a signature option. With such fresh food to choose from, there's no wrong selection. Fishbowl has grown rapidly from its original beachside location, with venues also in Darlinghurst, North Sydney, Manly, Surry Hills and the CBD.

FISHBOWLBONDI.COM.AU

GREEN DREAM

186 Campbell Pde, Bondi Beach

SERVING /

Juices
Salad Bar

SALAD DAYS • Not all salad bars are created equal, with limp ingredients and lack of substance the norm for many. Enter Green Dream: a venture from Fratelli Fresh founder Barry McDonald that lives up to its name as a champion of the good stuff. The bright and leafy venue on Bondi Beach offers a weekly menu of four 'Dream salads', derived from more than 50 ingredients and 13 dressing options. There's also the option to build your own salad creation, starting with a base of greens, quinoa or wild rice, then topped with up to five ingredients, such as tomato, edamame or corn, and a protein or healthy carbs like salmon or turmeric sweet potato. It's all about quality produce here, as the ingredients have nowhere to hide. No filler lettuce to be seen.

GREEN-DREAM.COM.AU

SIDE ROOM

180–186 Campbell Pde, Bondi Beach

SERVING /

Breakfast
Lunch
Acai Bowls
Whole Bowls
Smoothies

TASTY PITSHOP • Side Room is a casual hotspot from the minds behind poke eatery, Fishbowl, and renowned Potts Point cafe, Room 10. The concept offers smoothies, 'whole bowls', sandwiches, coffee and simple, delicious all-day breakfast, where you can make a leisurely pitstop or fuel up on the go with healthy, hearty fare. All ingredients are sourced locally and the food offering is well-executed, served in a fast, relaxed environment that's popular with take-away beach goers. The 20-seater dining space is minimalist, cool and welcoming, just a short walk to the shores of Bondi. Side Room's incorporation of specialty ingredients, superfoods, native herbs and spices have all contributed to its popularity and loyal customer base. With affordable, high-quality ingredients made in-house, Side Room has something for discerning palates, every day of the week.

VERD

Barangaroo, Manly & Surry Hills

SERVING /

Coffee
Breakfast
Lunch
Raw Treats
Smoothies

MARKET FRESH • Verd is a chain of plant-based salad bars aiming to provide healthy, fresh and sustainable food to communities across Sydney. Currently located in Barangaroo, Surry Hills and Manly, the Verd team aims to inspire Sydney-siders to go for healthy lunches and dinners that use the freshest, most vibrant, local ingredients.
They work with local providers to secure seasonal produce from the markets every morning to turn into delicious bowls packed with flavour. The team has also formed a relationship with small artisans who make products such as macadamia feta and fresh tofu from scratch with organic ingredients. Verd slices and dices the veggies fresh each morning to ensure they're still packed with nutrients and at their peak for taste. These meals are also available through delivery apps to ensure they're as accessible as possible.

 VERDSYDNEY.COM.AU

MODA

ACAI BROTHERS

Manly & Neutral Bay

SERVING /

Acai Bowls
Breakfast
Raw Treats
Coffee
Smoothies
Juices

FUN & FLAVOUR • The brainchild of two best friends, motivated to make health food readily available within their wider community, Acai Brothers Superfood Bar is one of Australia's fastest-growing superfood franchises. Founders Ben Day and Sam Carson have worked tirelessly to develop a menu that satisfies the taste buds of any food lover, offering seasonally changing menus that feature specialty acai bowls, juices, smoothies, raw treats and coffee. With over 25 locations nationwide, Acai Brothers is the healthy alternative to 'food on the go'. Day and Carson are driven to consistently provide the highest quality in superfoods on the market. They are passionate about re-inventing the concept of health food by injecting fun and flavour into the experience. Here, you can nourish yourself quickly with quality ingredients, which could lead to long-lasting changes.

ACAIBROTHERS.COM.AU

BARE NAKED BOWLS

Bronte, Dee Why Beach, Manly & Surry Hills

SERVING /

Acai Bowls
Raw Treats
Smoothies
Juices
Organic Coffee
Kombucha

BOWLS OF ENERGY • The name says it all: Bare Naked Bowls, one of Sydney's favourite superfood cafes, lets simplicity shine by using only fresh, seasonal and organic ingredients. Specialising in delicious acai bowls, superfood smoothies, breakfast bowls, cold-pressed juices, locally roasted coffee, kombucha and raw treats, the cafe caters to various diets including vegetarian, paleo, vegan, dairy-free and gluten-free. Bare Naked Bowls believes in living a conscious and active lifestyle and aims to deliver food that will give a healthy boost of energy. The selection of bowls will leave you feeling refreshed, energised and ready to take on the day. The cafe, which has four locations in Sydney, is proud to support IBSH, a charity that helps disadvantaged and orphaned children in developing nations to achieve tertiary education and better life opportunities.

BARENAKEDBOWLS.COM.AU

CALI PRESS

Bondi, Bronte, Coogee, Double Bay & Surry Hills

SERVING /

Breakfast
Lunch
Coffee
Cold Pressed Juices
Smoothies

NOT JUST JUICE • With five locations in Sydney – at Bondi, Bronte, Coogee, Double Bay and Surry Hills – Cali Press is a popular go-to for cold-pressed juices, smoothies and AllPress coffee. Each venue has a great range of organic wholefoods and snacks, as well as detox juice cleanse programs. From metabolic boosters to rich antioxidant detoxifiers, Cali Press' 100% raw, organic cold-pressed juices are essentially the freshest sourced raw fruit and vegetables in a bottle. Their market-leading juice cleanses are designed to detoxify while maintaining a healthy lifestyle. They apply a complete cold chain to ensure maximum retention of the vitamins, minerals and enzymes extracted from the organic produce. As well as being a dine-in cafe, Cali Press also offers a wonderful 'health shelf' range, specifically designed to grab-and-go, and is both nutritious and convenient.

CALIPRESS.COM.AU

CALI PRESS
COLD PRESSED JUICE

NAKED FOODS

Over 9 Stores in Sydney

PRODUCTS /

Beans & Lentils
Kombucha on Tap
Local Honey
Locally Sourced Nuts
Natural Beauty
Vegan Chocolates
Roasted Nut Butters
Superfoods

STRIPPED BACK • Naked Foods Organic Health Foods is all about 'taking it all off' and shedding the weight of today's often-unhealthy diets of processed and polluted food. Founded in 2012 by entrepreneur Caique Ponzoni, Naked Foods started at Sydney farmers markets before expanding to meet the appetite from Aussies to eat better, be more informed and do their part to reduce their environmental impact. Naked Foods Organic Health Foods sources natural food direct from nature, without the unwanted dressings of modern processing. Their packaging is simple and sustainable – brown paper bags, filled by scoop from bulk drums, then weighed and sold. Customers are rewarded for moving towards a zero waste lifestyle: using your own packaging allows for a 5% discount. The company is constantly seeking ways to become more sustainable, from suppliers, to in-store practices.

WHOLEFOODS HOUSE

Rosebery & Woollahra

PRODUCTS /

Organic & Biodynamic
Fruit & Vegetables
Organic Meats
Seafood
Wholefoods

COMMUNITY SPIRIT • Wholefoods House is a family-owned and operated business that opened its first store in Woollahra in 2004. Following its success, they opened a second store in Waterloo in 2007, which relocated to the Cannery in Rosebery in mid-2017. Both locations offer a comprehensive range of organic and natural products alongside an abundant range of Australian-grown certified organic produce. At Wholefoods House, they pride themselves on offering a complete range of fresh produce and wholesome food, with wonderful staff, inspiring suppliers and valued customers counted as part of their community. They are committed to supplying only the best-available fresh produce, which means early morning runs to the organic markets a few times a week to hand-pick orders. The business supports local, ethical and artisan producers and buys direct from them wherever possible.

WHOLEFOODSHOUSE.COM.AU

HEALTH FOOD STORES /

When you're looking for an obscure supplement, a specialty ingredient or perhaps an aspirational browse, a health food store is the place to be. Boost or kickstart your wellness journey with these wonderful options.

ABOUT LIFE
Rozelle & Surry Hills

ALFALFA HOUSE
113 Enmore Road, Newtown

BONDI WHOLE FOODS
North Bondi & Surry Hills

FLANNERY'S
Bondi Junction, Cronulla, Crows Nest, Lane Cove & Mona Vale

FRUITOLOGIST
Bondi & Rozelle

HARRIS FARM
Bondi Beach, Bondi Junction, Broadway, Cammeray, Drummoyne, Edgecliff, Leichhardt, Lindfield, Manly, Mona Vale, Mosman, Potts Point & Randwick

MANLY FARM ORGANIC GROCER
17-25 Wentworth St, Manly

MANLY FOOD CO-OPERATIVE
11-25 Wentworth St, Manly

NAKED FOODS
Bondi Junction, Brookvale, Cronulla, Double Bay, Manly, Mosman, Newtown, Northbridge & Tramsheds

OFARM
34 Old Pittwater Rd, Brookvale

SCOOP WHOLEFOODS
180 Campbell Pde, Bondi Beach

THE HEALTH EMPORIUM
263-265 Bondi Rd, Bondi

TASTE ORGANIC
Crows Nest, Enmore & Turramurra

THE SOURCE BULK FOODS
Balgowlah, Balmain, Crows Nest, Glebe, Lane Cove, North Willoughby, Rhodes & Zetland

UMU
81a Gould St, Bondi Beach

WHOLEFOODS HOUSE
Rosebery & Woollahra

[THE WELL - BONDI BEACH]

FARMERS MARKETS /

Sydneysiders love a good farmers market and supply certainly keeps up with demand. Whether you're seeking beautiful organic produce, handmade wares, here are some of the city's best options.

BONDI FARMERS MARKET
Campbell Parade, Bondi Beach
Sat: 9am - 1pm

CAMBRIDGE MARKETS EQ
122 Lang Rd, Moore Park
Wed & Sat: 8am - 2pm

CARRIAGEWORKS
245 Wilson St, Eveleigh
Sat: 8am - 1pm

FRENCHS FOREST ORGANIC MARKET
5 Frenchs Forest Rd, Frenchs Forest
Sun: 9am - 1pm

GROWERS MARKET
Pyrmont Bay Park, Pyrmont
4th Saturday of each month: 7:30am - 12pm

KINGS CROSS ORGANIC FOOD MARKETS
Fitzroy Gardens, Potts Point
Sun: 10am - 3pm

NORTHSIDE PRODUCE MARKET
200 Miller St, North Sydney
1st & 3rd Saturday of every month:

ORGANIC MARKET
142 Addison Rd, Marrickville
Sun: 9am - 3pm

ORANGE GROVE
2-8 Perry St, Lilyfield
Sat: 8am - 1pm

RAMSGATE ORGANIC MARKET
Ramsgate Public School, Ramsgate Beach. Sat: 8am - 2pm

SYDNEY SUSTAINABLE MARKETS
Taylor Sq, Darlinghurst
Sat: 8am - 1pm

SYDNEY VEGAN MARKETS
122 Lang Rd, Moore Park
3rd Sunday of every month

THE ROCKS MARKET
Jack Mundey Place, The Rocks
Sat & Sun: 10am - 5pm

JESSICA SEPEL /

Jessica Sepel is a clinical nutritionist, best-selling author, international health blogger and the voice behind JSHealth and @jshealth. She is passionate about helping people overcome fad dieting and disordered eating, having gone through her own struggles with food. Her philosophy is focused around balance, rest and building a healthy relationship with food.

TELL US ABOUT YOUR LIFE JOURNEY AND HOW THIS INSPIRED YOU TO START JS HEALTH.

Just a few years ago, I felt totally disconnected from my own body and alone in my thoughts. At age 14, I discovered diets and became an obsessive fad dieter for years, to the point where I was verging on a serious eating disorder. This way of thinking was my 'normal' and I couldn't see past it.

During that time, my self-esteem was shot. I lost too much weight, too quickly and then that number on the scale would yo-yo. Since I could never maintain the 'perfect' diet or 'ideal' weight – which I now know don't exist – I was caught in a toxic cycle. Food governed my life in an unhealthy way, and I tormented myself by bingeing and then restricting myself with food.

I thought that being thin would make me more lovable. Looking back, it had the opposite effect: it didn't make me feel any more loved by others, and I definitely didn't love myself. I used food to reward and punish myself and always compared myself to others. I channelled all that self-hate into my body, and my body became my biggest burden.

It was time-consuming, stressful, and incredibly exhausting. On the outside, I 'had it all', but the sad thing was, the amazing things about my life didn't matter because I was distracted by the endless and futile pursuit to be perfect.

Then, something clicked. I realised hating on my body was affecting everything, so I committed to understanding what nutrition was all about. When I learnt how the body actually works, my mentality changed.

Fast forward to now: I'm a completely different person. I've taken control of my life, my eating habits and my thoughts. I studied nutrition for five years: I completed a Bachelor of Health and then two years of Nutritional Medicine. I remember sitting in my nutrition lectures being absolutely blown away by what I was learning. That feeling hasn't changed. I began experimenting with wholefoods, and shifting my mindset to be more positive. And slowly, I started healing my relationship with my body.

This is when I started writting about my journey in a blog - from fad dieter to wholefood eater. I named the blog JSHealth and from then onwards I created a platform for women to come together and support each other to live a healthier and more balanced life.

WHAT WAS IT LIKE TO START JSHEALTH?

It was a total accident. It was scary and daunting, but it was meant to be. I was just blogging about my journey and experience; I had no desire to do anything more with it. I just wanted to be a nutritionist in private practice. JSHealth as the brand took off organically. I think women can just relate to the realness of it.

AND WHAT HAS BEEN THE BIGGEST CHALLENGE?

I had to give up private practice, which was hard because I loved it. But the business of JSHealth just took up too much time and mental capacity. The challenge is still feeling quite exposed. Having a presence on social media comes with a lot of pressure.

HOW HAS A FAILURE, OR APPARENT FAILURE, SET YOU UP FOR LATER SUCCESS?

You have to see failure as part of this journey. I'm OK with it. Every single project we have created has come with immense challenges. We have had to pull the plug on certain projects, which could be seen as a failure. But instead I have chosen to see it as 'it just wasn't meant to be'. The trick is to keep going when challenge or failure hits. Once you pass that, success will come.

TACTICS, ROUTINES AND HABITS /

WHAT DOES THE FIRST HOUR OF YOUR MORNING ROUTINE LOOK LIKE?

I wake up and do a gratitude practice. I make a piccolo coffee, practice yoga, take my probiotic and enjoy a JSHealth breakfast. The biggest trick is I won't let myself check social media or emails under after my morning routine.

WHAT IS THE BEST OR MOST WORTHWHILE INVESTMENT YOU'VE EVER MADE?

My best investment is focusing all my love, time and care on the JSHealth community. I truly care about them. My focus has always been on the people, not the numbers.

WHAT NEW BELIEF, BEHAVIOUR, OR HABIT HAS MOST IMPROVED YOUR LIFE?

Learning that things take time. Not everything can happen immediately. The slower, the better.

WHAT IS THE BOOK (OR BOOKS) YOU'VE GIVEN AS A GIFT, AND WHY?

You Can Heal Your Life by Louise Hay - sounds a little corny but the principles in this book changes my perspective and mentality, from negative to positive, from lack to abundance.

WHAT IS YOUR BEST TIP FOR FEELING GOOD?

Relieve the pressure to do it all right, to do it all perfectly. Take it one step at a time.

[PARAMOUNT RECREATION CLUB – SURRY HILLS]

FITNESS

FITNESS STUDIOS. HEALTH CLUBS
YOGA. PILATES. BARRE FITNESS
INDOOR CYCLING. OUTDOOR SPACES

LA PORTE WELLNESS

87-103 Epsom Rd, Rosebery

SERVICES /

Infrared Sauna
Meditation
Pilates
Yoga

ONE-STOP LUXURY • La Porte Group's concept space, La Porte Wellness, brings together leading innovators in Pilates, yoga, wellness, beauty and skincare, under one very stylish roof. The architecturally designed, Scandinavian-style complex includes world-class reformer and mat Pilates studios, infrared sauna studios, and the 10th luxury flagship for renowned Australian skincare brand Rationale, as well as celebrity brow and lash technician, Kristin Fisher. The space's Wellness Collective includes regular guest contributors who specialise in meditation, yoga, boxing, kinesiology and healing massage. La Porte Wellness also offers a healthy menu for its guests and permanent residents, which includes detoxifying juices and teas from Orchard St. and delicious food designed by plant-based cafe, YOUENI. The entire experience helps you to nourish and revive your body, soul and mind.

LAPORTESPACE.COM.AU

PARAMOUNT RECREATION CLUB

80 Commonwealth St, Surry Hills

SERVICES /

Fitness
Massage
Meditation
Chiropractor
Dietetics

GO TO THE TOP • Far from the standard musty gym, Paramount Recreation Club is set on one of the most beautiful rooftops in Sydney, and brings together physical, mental and social health for a well-rounded approach to modern living. The fitness offering is built around three key pillars: strength, movement and conditioning. Under the guidance of some of Sydney's best specialist instructors, the 'Rec Club' offers a weekly schedule of more than 100 classes that include yoga, mat pilates, barre, Olympic lifting, boxing, skipping, meditation as well as the signature 'Paramount workout'. To complement the fitness program, the club offers integrated health services including massage, dietetics and personalised health assessments. Members can also book private or small-group training with a member from the experienced team.

PARAMOUNTRECREATION.CLUB

SPEEDO FITNESS CLUB

180 Campbell Ave, Bondi Beach

SERVICES /

Group Fitness
Heated Pool
Open Plan Studio
24/7 Access

FULL-SERVICE FACILITY • Speedo Fitness Club is proud to be the first and only gym in Bondi Beach that offers 24/7 access, allowing you to train at your own convenience. The club also features the suburb's only indoor heated pool - a 25m custom-designed variety - as well as leading innovations and state-of-the art cardio and strength equipment from Technogym. Apart from the cutting-edge gym facilities, there's also a beautiful open-plan studio offering group classes, including HIIT, BodyPump, Boxercise, yoga, Pilates, barre and Zumba. There's also aqua aerobics, exclusive Spin H2O and swim programs available in the pool. An experienced team of personal trainers can help you leverage the facilities to get best results. SFC combines the opportunities of a full-service health club, with the luxury, intimate DNA of a boutique gym experience.

SPEEDOFITNESSCLUB.COM

VIRGIN ACTIVE

400 Barangaroo Ave, Barangaroo

SERVICES /

Personal Training
Indoor Cycle
Strength & Cardio
Boxing

NEXT LEVEL • Virgin Active is all about irresistible exercise experiences. They go to extraordinary lengths to deliver something unexpectedly better, and very different – a 'global facility concept'. From a concierge to greet you by name and take care of the little things, to rockstar instructors tailoring your workout on the ground, this is a next-level fitness experience. Book your favourite bike or bag, and the team will have your cycle shoes or ozone-cleaned leather boxing gloves ready and waiting on arrival. Virgin Active's new Revolution cycle, Focus boxing, Burn strength and cardio, and outdoor Calibration programs are inspired by the leading boutiques of the world, but Australian made. They know you're busy and exercise has to fit around you, so every program is scheduled multiple times a day. They're big on the little things.

VIRGINACTIVE.COM.AU

98 GYM

98 Riley St, Darlinghurst

SERVICES /

Group Glasses
Personal Training

STRENGTH AND SPIRIT • Home to some of Australia's leading strength and conditioning coaches, 98 Gym builds resilience and values integrity, persistence and hard work over aesthetics and ego. At 98, highly qualified and experienced trainers always want more from your performance, and their own, both physically and mentally. They approach time in the gym in the same way they approach every aspect of their lives. Under pressure, they believe you'll only ever be as good as your training. That's why they train so hard, to build resilience that translates into daily life. Group classes at 98 feature comprehensive and progressive goal-based strength and conditioning programming, ensuring that clients continuously improve over time. All classes are programmed by the team of respected trainers, who have a range of backgrounds - from former elite athletes, to members of the defence force.

98GYM.COM

98 GYM

AGOGA

164 Bondi Rd, Bondi

SERVICES /

Group Training
Health Coaching
Personal Training

LEANER, FASTER, STRONGER • Agōga (pronounced ah-go-jyah) is a Spartan word for the education and training regimen used to create "a class of warrior citizens" – strong of mind, unflinchingly loyal and physically unmatched. Just like the athletes and warriors of old, the Agōga team believes in training our bodies the way nature intended. We were born to move – to run, jump, lift and climb in response to our environment. This is called functional training and it's at the heart of all Agōga classes. Their functional training is all about multi-plane movement. Unlike traditional programs, which focus on working specific muscles, it works on often-limited planes of motion, which will improve your health and athleticism. Combined with effective HIIT and strength training, Agōga creates natural, symmetrical bodies, improves mobility, fascia health, acceleration and speed, and builds strength and power.

ATHLETES AUTHORITY

4 Cleg St, Artarmon

SERVICES /

Athlete Development
Athlete Mentorship
Gym Memberships

WORLD-CLASS FACILITY • At Athletes Authority, you're joining the only gym in Sydney that's built just for athletes. They train team sport, individuals, weightlifting and powerlifting to perform at a higher level and achieve what may seem impossible. The Athletes Authority team designed the gym from the ground up, to create a facility that was customised specifically for athletes, not just to accommodate them. They went above and beyond to get the best equipment, coaching and advice that creates world-class athletes. Since opening, they've changed the lives of more than 200 athletes and created a unique, supportive, like-minded community. Their mission is to help you become the best athlete you've ever been by getting access to a high-performance facility when you need it most.

ATHLETESAUTHORITY.ORG

BARRY'S BOOTCAMP

Martin Place & Surry Hills

SERVICES /

Group Classes (HIIT)

HIGH ACHIEVERS • Barry's is the premier high-intensity immersive workout phenomenon that launched a global fitness revolution. Since its inception in Los Angeles in 1998, with over 20 years of expert development, Barry's champions a highly effective combination of High Intensity Interval Training (HIIT) through 55-minute classes. Each class, incorporates 25 minutes of interval-based cardiovascular routines on the specially designed Barry's Woodway treadmills, with a further 25 minutes of strength and conditioning using free weights, resistance bands and more, followed by a five-minute cool-down. The Barry's program is designed to tone muscle, incinerate fat by burning up to 1000 calories, and create a spike in metabolism for up to 48 hours after. Led by the Sydney founding instructors, the CBD studio schedule is customised to focus on independent muscle groups each day of the week.

BARRYSBOOTCAMP.COM

WELCOME
TO BARRYS
AUSTRALIA
BARRYS
X
MID

BEAT BODY

248 Palmer St, Darlinghurst

SERVICES /

Group Classes
(HIIT, Boxing, Stretching)

FEEL THE BEAT • At Beat Body, they've created a unique space for you to sweat. Uplifting instructors use beat-based playlists to help drive your full-body workout to a new high. Their three signature workouts, Beat, Box and Breathe, find the perfect balance to give you a complete fitness experience. Beat combines cardio, strength, bodyweight exercises and core, while Box infuses boxing with lower body movements to the beat of the music. Breathe is a chance to slow down and escape the day to day. Tone, stretch and meditate through the playlist and find your mellow state. Each class consists of 10 songs and last roughly 45 minutes. There is also an in-house nutritionist to help you get the results you desire, in the right headspace to make long-lasting changes.

BEATBODY.COM

BEAT BOD

BIKINI BODS

Brookvale, CBD, Mona Vale & North Sydney

SERVICES /

Personal Training
Boxing Classes
Functional Classes
Muay Thai Kickboxing
Women's Only Studio
Apparel
Boxing Gear

OUTSIDE THE BOX • Bikini Bods is about strengthening and empowering women with a supportive community, unique fitness programs and dedicated motivational coaches. Their specialty styles of non-contact Muay Thai kickboxing fitness, boxing fitness, high intensity interval training and bodyweight circuit training have been specifically designed for women. The sessions will improve lean muscle, fat loss and cardiovascular endurance, resulting in amazing body transformations. All the Sydney studios welcome and encourage women of all ages, fitness levels and experience. Every class is suitable for beginners and allow you to go at your own pace to progressively improve. Bikini Bods instructors use various combinations of kickboxing, boxing and circuits to ensure all workouts are challenging and never the same.

BIKINIBODS.COM.AU

BUF GIRLS STUDIO

204 Bondi Rd, Bondi

SERVICES /

Group Training
Health Coaching
Personal Training
Speaking Events

CELEBRATING WOMEN • BUF Girls was designed to create a comfortable, welcoming environment for women to train alongside each other in a beautiful, like-minded community. Being a 'BUF Girl' isn't about competition, body image or comparison; it's about friendship and community, healthy bodies and healthy minds. It's about inspiring, supporting and celebrating each other and forgetting about chasing a shallow ideal of beauty. It's about training for how it makes you feel: happy, healthy, balanced, alert, calm, centred, strong, powerful, beautiful, unstoppable and fearless. Training at either the brand new studio on Bondi Road, or at various locations at Bondi Beach, expect epic workouts set to fun DJ-mixed beats and a whole lot of good vibes.

BUFGIRLS.COM

WHO RUN THE WORLD? GIRLS!
WHO RUN THE WORLD? GIRLS!

BY FITNESS PLAYGROUND

THE RIGHT FIT /

Have you tried bootcamps, training programs and classes with mixed results? Fitness can be a journey of trial and error, but if backed by great people, you'll progress to success. Here's how to find the right trainer for you.

WHAT IS IT ABOUT PAYING $200 A MONTH TO RUN AROUND IN THE RAIN, COLD OR DARKNESS WITH MINIMAL EQUIPMENT THAT KEEPS PEOPLE GOING BACK FOR MORE?

And what is it that makes them choose that over training in a gym with the best equipment and facilities at a quarter of the price?

ONE WORD: COMMUNITY.

Community drives fitness success: harnessing motivation and delivering results by making you feel part of something bigger than yourself. Having people who care about who you are and the journey you're on is what will get you to the gym, even on the days you don't really want to be there. It's that consistency and positive relationship with exercise that will get you the long-lasting results you're looking for.

So, if you want to be successful on your fitness journey, find a place where you belong, surrounded by great people who inspire you and those that make you actually enjoy exercise, not just tolerate it.

Our focus at Fitness Playground was to create the bootcamp mentality in a gym environment. Personal trainers can be a great bridge towards integrating yourself into gym life. They're ever present – engaging with members, energising the gym floor and creating a culture where every interaction is valued and long-term relationships can flourish. But it's important to choose the right one.

SO, HOW DO YOU KNOW WHAT TO LOOK FOR – OR AVOID?

The fitness industry is saturated with trainers who have the 'machine gun mentality': they will unload 1000 bullets in the hope that one of them hits their target. We believe in the 'sniper mentality' – taking the time to gather all necessary information before taking the shot.

You need to start with a trainer who is a great person first, because no amount of education can replace a genuine passion and care toward helping others thrive. It's important for your trainer to take the time to get to know every piece of relevant information about you, considering all the variables to create a fitness plan bespoke to your wants and needs. Not just a 'one size fits all'.

Fitness is about more than just a quick fix; it's a lifestyle change to keep you always moving forward and set up for long-term success.

THEFITNESSPLAYGROUND.COM.AU

THE BUNKER

69-81 Foveaux St, Surry Hills

SERVICES /

Group Training
Personal Trainers
Aerial Yoga
Barre
Pilates
24/7

ESCAPE LIFE • At The Bunker, you're invited to descend below the city streets to enter a futuristic world of raw concrete, neon lights and brushed metal – a motivating space to step outside your comfort zone. Ready to train like an athlete? The Bunker will challenge you to find another version of yourself and change your training forever. It's a gym with an unparalleled offering: from super-ergonomic Atlantis strength machines to a primal class allowing you to master the art of movement, you'll be pushed to the limit by trainers who faced a rigorous hiring process. An extensive range of group classes include gymnastic strength, Barbell, Badass, Krav Maga, Pilates, Strongman, handstands, aerial yoga, barre and meditation. There's also expert personal training available. The Bunker's motto is: "don't get bored, get results."

THEBUNKERGYM.COM.AU

THE BUNKER
THE BUNKER
MATRIX

CREATURE FITNESS

Bondi Junction, Edgecliff & Marrickville

SERVICES /

CrossFit
Community Social
Events
Lifestyle Management
Nutrition Coaching
Private Coaching
Small Group Classes

COMMITTED COMMUNITY • Creature Fitness is a premium training facility that helps successful professionals excel beyond their current fitness level. Their method involves high-level coaching, a positive community, and smart and fun programming. Since 2014, across three locations in the heart of Sydney, Creature has been re-inventing CrossFit training for its clients, offering exclusive coaching from world-class professionals with individualised nutrition principles, healthy lifestyle habits and movement patterns. Creature provide a tailored approach for the committed professional who is willing to put the work in to achieve exceptional results. They understand the importance of time and make sure its used wisely to make the most of every session. There's a range of group classes available, or you can start your journey with a dedicated fitness professional.

CREATUREFITNESS.COM.AU

CREW BOUTIQUE ROWING STUDIO

428 George St, Sydney

SERVICES /

Group Classes
Personal Training
Corporate Fitness

JOIN THE CREW • CREW Row is a boutique rowing studio. Their effective fitness classes are centered around the gracefully hand-crafted timber WaterRower, burning calories in every stroke with the soothing sound of moving water. This unique, full-body circuit class keeps the heart rate pumping while placing minimal impact on your body. Within 45 minutes you will have worked all of your major muscle groups – everything from your arms, legs, back and core are engaged. CREW also uses high-intensity interval training, with workstations focusing on toning, sculpting and strengthening exercises. Fast transitions between the rowing machine and the floor will ensure you are never in the same spot for too long. By combining rowing with dumbbells, resistance bands, medicine balls and other equipment, you will increase both your muscular strength and endurance while making your workout fun and effective.

CREWROW.COM.AU

THE CUBE GYM

134-140 Old Pittwater Rd, Brookvale

SERVICES /

- Group Classes
- Personal Training
- Exercise Physiology
- Female Only Classes
- Physiotherapy
- Yoga

GOAL ORIENTED • At The Cube Gym, they aspire to create a positive team environment that builds a sense of community while helping build functional health and fitness. There's more than 35 group classes available each week, from HIIT circuits, strength and conditioning and ladies-only workouts, to strongman sessions, boxing and yoga. The classes are programmed and coached by highly experienced industry professionals who work with members to get the best out of their session – no matter their level of experience, fitness or gym know-how. There are also personal trainers on hand for tailored individual programs, or semi-private training with small groups for more customised sessions. The Cube Gym also offers personal training, exercise physiology and physiotherapy for those with more specific goals or injury rehabilitation needs. No matter your goals, you'll find the right guidance.

THECUBEGYM.COM.AU

EMBODY

155 Military Rd, Neutral Bay

SERVICES /

Barre
Meditation
Personal Training
Pilates
Tai Chi
Yoga

TRANSFORM YOURSELF • Embody is an urban sanctuary where you can become the happiest, healthiest and fittest version of yourself. Their focus is on a holistic approach to health and wellbeing that allows you to achieve the best result for your individual goals. The unique Embody Method philosophy concentrates on achieving wellbeing through physical, mental, and emotional fitness. Intent on ensuring all aspects of wellness, Embody's carefully chosen instructors and personal trainers have undertaken their own Embody transformations. With their guidance, you can achieve body confidence, flexibility and strength, as well as a healthy 'unplugged' mentality, and a nutritional education that will inform sustainable, long-term lifestyle changes. Embody's mission is to ensure you look and feel your best.

EMBODY.COM.AU

ENLIVEN COACHING

117 Old Pittwater Rd, Brookvale

SERVICES /

Group Classes
Personal Training
Corporate Training
Mums & Bubs

FUN FITNESS • Smiling faces. Electric, uplifting atmosphere. A sense of comradeship. Badass workouts. Zero mediocrity. That's what you can expect at Enliven Coaching. The difference is clear and that's why Enliven is quickly becoming the largest independent gym on the Northern Beaches. There's a range of classes for men and women, from fat-burning weights to mixed martial arts-inspired HIIT, Pilates, boxing, and the newest addition, Flatline. The trainers are industry experts putting the 'personal' back into personal trainer. They care about your results and will push you to your limits to get them. Each class is diverse and empowering, so you'll leave the gym feeling nothing less than inspired and accomplished. Enliven's signature 10-week educational programs raise money and awareness for different community initiatives such as Bears of Hope, Do it for Dolly Foundation and Livin Suicide Prevention.

VEN COA

FALSEGRIP

19 Cross St, Brookvale

SERVICES /

- Group Class Training
- Private Training
- Private Groups
- Youth Programs
- Events
- Workshops

REBUILD YOUR BODY • Falsegrip pioneered adult gymnastics strength training in Sydney, creating a unique and fun style that builds strength, mobility and flexibility - no matter your age or fitness level. They offer classes for beginners right through to experienced athletes, so you'll always find something that's right for you. Falsegrip's team of specialised coaches understand how to use exercise to rebuild your body from head to toe, with a focus on the health of your joints and connective tissues. When you join the studio in Northern Beaches, you'll find a community of people who are driven to challenge their bodies and minds every time they visit, as well as unique gymnastics equipment you won't often find in other gyms. Falsegrip is more than a workout, it's a lifestyle change; a new approach to training that will transform the way you move, feel and live.

FALSEGRIP.COM.AU

#falsegrip

[SKIN THE CAT]

BY FALSEGRIP

BODY LANGUAGE /

Gymnastics isn't based upon the movement of individual muscles; it's about how those parts of the body speak to each other to work as a whole. Falsegrip explains how to harness a holistic approach for long-term results.

FLEXIBILITY VS. MOBILITY

Being flexible isn't enough. We can define flexibility as a person's passive range of motion, whereas mobility is their ability to actively achieve a range of motion. For example, flexibility would be a dancer sitting on the floor in the splits; mobility would be that same dancer, standing and lifting one leg in the air into a splits position.

Improving mobility requires hard work and patience. We must first aim to achieve a desired passive range of motion (ROM), then work to develop strength in and control over as much of that newly acquired ROM as possible. This is mobility. When stretching for the first time (and we mean really stretching, not just spending 10 seconds before going for a jog), you might decide that it's quite uncomfortable - please don't give up. If you're tight or immobile, take a moment to think about how many years it took for you to become that way. It's going to take time for your body, specifically your nervous system, to adapt to its new range of motion and begin to feel comfortable in and have control over those new positions.

CONSISTENCY VS. INTENSITY

Focusing on being consistent with your training is far more valuable than focusing on the intensity.

Too much high intensity training isn't sustainable in the long run, as the cumulative stress on the body eventually results in it feeling depleted and unable to recover sufficiently to adapt and improve. In the short term, this may mean you aren't even able to train the following day. Someone who trains at an intensity level suitable for them to recover and train again the following day — and the day after that — will, through consistency, complete a much higher volume of training and achieve better results over time.

A COMBINED APPROACH

Falsegrip's training method works to build strength, mobility and flexibility throughout your entire body. Our focus on improving mobility first and building strong healthy joints, that move the way they're supposed to, works to 'bulletproof' the body and reduce your risk of injury. This means less downtime and more of what you love, inside and outside of the gym.

The more strength and usable ROM you possess, the more freedom you have to pursue the exciting stuff like handstands. It's important to keep goals exciting.

Our group training environment is built upon a strong community vibe, where members interact with and support one another to help reach their goals. With increased movement potential, body awareness and body control, also comes increased self-confidence, which improves the ability to make and maintain social connections and contributes to positive emotional and mental wellbeing.

GOOD GOALS FOR BEGINNERS

First, aim to overcome strength and mobility deficits. This will then enable you to perform basic human movements such as squatting, hanging, jumping and push/pull movements without pain or restriction.

With consistent training and having achieved these fundamental movements as a base for you to build upon, we recommend aiming toward these five goals in your first 12 months:

PANCAKE (sitting on the floor with your legs outstretched and hands in front of you, aiming to flatten your back and get your chest on the floor)

FREESTANDING HANDSTAND (10 seconds)

BRIDGE (otherwise known as a backbend)

RING MUSCLE-UP (strict)

COSSACK SQUAT (most of your weight is on one leg while the other leg is kept out straight and to the side.)

FALSEGRIP /

Falsegrip offer adult gymnastics classes in Brookvale for beginners through to experienced athletes, so you'll always find something that's right for you. Their team of specialised coaches understand how to use exercise to rebuild your body from head to toe, with a focus on the health of your joints and connective tissues.

FALSEGRIP.COM.AU

[FREESTANDING HANDSTAND]

FITNESS PLAYGROUND

Surry Hills, Marrickville & Newtown

SERVICES /

Group Training
Personal Trainers
Aerial Yoga
Barre
Pilates

GET IN THE GAME • Remember when you loved running around and being active? Well, Fitness Playground is taking you back there. Since opening in 2014 to create a fun, friendly gym environment, they've expanded to multiple locations, thousands of members and over 100 staff. Their trainers are put through their paces – five rounds, to be exact – before they're chosen to join the team. Classes vary from circus-inspired aerial movement, Pilates, yoga and barre, to intense and technical kickboxing, indoor cycling and dance flow. There's a vast range to choose from, no matter your mood or fitness level. The mind is also covered with meditation sessions to refocus. It's a playground for everyone, no matter your destination or experience level. Whether you're a newbie yogini, a ninja warrior or a calisthenics guru, Fitness Playground is committed to revolutionising your gym experience.

THEFITNESSPLAYGROUND.COM.AU

FLOW ATHLETIC

134 Oxford St, Paddington

SERVICES /

Personal Training
Indoor Cycling
Yoga Studio

POWER OF THREE • Flow Athletic is a complete workout experience in the heart of Paddington that takes a balanced approach to fitness. They recommend members follow the 'Flow philosophy' of 1:1:1 – one strength session, either Strength-Strong or barre; one cardio session, including spin, boxing or a run class; and one yoga session, which provides a chance to stretch, breathe and meditate. This method allows clients to get the best physical and mental results from their training, with the least chance of injury, and lends itself to greater longevity in the program and beyond. Flow's large, award-winning studio has three luxe custom spaces for the different session types, allowing you to bend, lift and sweat in style. There's also a client lounge, high-end changeroom facilities, free lockers and an in-body scan service available.

FLOWATHLETIC.COM.AU/

JUNGLE BROTHERS

15 Underwood Ave, Botany

SERVICES /

Group Training
Personal Training
Sports Massage
Custom Programming

FIND YOUR TRIBE • The Jungle Brothers is a 'tribe' of like-minded humans joining together on a journey of development and evolution. They recognise a mismatch between the way homo sapiens evolved to exist, and the way the modern world is now shaping us to be – and believe repairing this misalignment will yield better people and a better world. So, how? By vowing to diminish harmful practices in the fitness industry and build skilful, strong and mobile humans. Their training method embraces three spheres of practice: lift, fight and move, in patterns, environments and scenarios our bodies were designed for. No prior experience is required to join The Jungle Brothers tribe. They pride themselves on working with people of all age ranges and abilities, and welcoming them fully into a fun, challenging and inclusive community.

JUNGLEBROTHERS.COM

LEAN BEAN FITNESS

11 Curlewis St, Bondi Beach

SERVICES /

Girls Only Studio
Group Classes
Personal Training
Retreats

KEEN AS A BEAN • Lean Bean Fitness is one of Sydney's favourite destinations for female fitness. Classes are uniquely choreographed by experienced instructors who have backgrounds in yoga, HIIT, barre and Pilates. All classes are based on continuous functional body weight movement, with plenty of variety provided by the BarreBeans, PowerBeans, BeanStrong (TRX) and BeanBox classes on offer. There are also 30-minute HIIT express classes to deliver maximum burn in minimum time for busy beans. A typical 'Lean Bean' is a 'fun-loving, fearless, and fabulous' female who likes to work hard but play a little harder. She loves the physical and mental challenge of an intense workout, but also knows when to chill out and have fun. She knows that the hardest part is always the showing up, and once the class starts, it's over before they know it.

LEANBEANFITNESS.COM

LIFT PERFORMANCE CENTRE

78-80 George St, Redfern

SERVICES /

Personal Training
Powerlifting Club
Group Classes
Cardio Room
Inbody Scanner
Sports Massage

HIGH ACHIEVERS • Lift Performance Centre is an impressive space, housed in a 120-year-old brick building and former art space, filled with natural light, exposed beams and five-metre-high ceilings. They spared no expense in cherry-picking the best equipment from around the world, including thick rotating grip Pro dumbbells; specialty bars and machines from the UK's, Watson; competition weightlifting and powerlifting bars and plates, and racks and bars from Sweden's, Eleiko, and more. The custom gymnastics fitout includes parallel bars, competition rings, wall bars and much more from Gymnova in France. Awarded *Men's Health Magazine* Australia's Best New Independent Gym award in 2015, Lift doesn't rest on its laurels. It was born out of a passion to provide best-quality training, in the best possible training environment, with the most welcoming and supportive community. An ideal they keep fighting for.

LIFTPERFORMANCECENTRE.COM

ALL BATTLES
ARE FIRST
WON OR LOST
IN THE MIND
LION BRAND

OF CROTON
600 BC

RUSHCUTTERS HEALTH

100 Bayswater Rd, Rushcutters Bay

SERVICES /

Personal Training
Small Group Classes
Programming
Apparel

PROVEN RESULTS • The team at Rushcutters Health specialises in offering the smartest nutritional guidance and individually prescribed training programs for its clients, with accountability from experienced coaches and support from a strong community of like-minded people. When starting a new program, the team will take you through a series of body composition tests to ensure that you not only 'feel better' from training, but also have key objective benchmarks for comparison along the way. The assessment also includes a thorough movement screen to test for muscle imbalance and mobility. By working with you to gather information on your goal, previous experience, injuries, food preferences and lifestyle, they can tailor a specific eating and exercise program you'll enjoy, that will deliver proven results. Lose body fat and gain strength, fitness, confidence and wellbeing.

RUSHCUTTERSHEALTH.COM.AU

30

TRUE

A SQUAD CALLED SAVAGE

11, 23-31 Darlinghurst Rd, Potts Point

SERVICES /

Group Classes
Personal Training
Boxing
Strength Training

SQUAD GOALS • Lead by Justin Savage, the Savage Training team specialises in training men and women of all fitness levels. Their studios and bootcamps have helped clients from all over the world, including the corporate world, with Linkedin in Sydney and Melbourne. Savage Training is passionate about educating men and women on how to workout, eat healthily, get in shape and maintain it for life. They aim to help you nourish, nurture and love your body so you can live a happy, healthy and fulfilling life. They've tried and tested many of the popular training fads and experimented with all types of food and know what works and what doesn't. The Savage system is simple and effective, with guaranteed results. Whether you prefer personal training, group training, bootcamp or online training, there's a package or service available for you.

SAVAGETRAINING.COM.AU

MARK BREWER /

Mark doesn't train everybody and he doesn't try to relate to everyone. He's focused on his passion to progress the traditions and professionalism of elite fighters with professional support, guidance and services. As a Judo competitor at the 2014 Glasgow Commonwealth Games, and in the pursuit of the Olympic podium, he brings a wealth of experience to strength and conditioning for fighters. Mark is on a mission to support fighters around the world. As host of the Fighters Performance Podcast, he is able to unite the fight community and provide free resources to support an elite performance.

TELL US ABOUT YOUR LIFE JOURNEY AS AN ATHLETE AND HOW THIS INSPIRED YOU TO START FIGHTERS PERFORMANCE?

My dream was to fight for gold at the Olympics, although every opportunity I had of making the Games died in vain due to lack of vital resources as an amateur athlete.

I had followed Strength and Conditioning as a career because I knew I would require the knowledge to see my body perform at its best.

While travelling the world for Judo, I was lucky enough to train and compete with the best teams and fighters around the world. Through these experiences, I realised how much of this professional approach to performance was lacking for amateur and unfunded fighters, worldwide.

Fighters Performance provides knowledge, guidance and services for fighters to perform at an elite level to ensure they don't stumble on the same cycle of underperformance and obstacles short of their dream, as I did.

WHAT WAS IT LIKE TO START FIGHTERS PERFORMANCE?

After retiring from competitive sport I pursued my career in Strength and Conditioning in the attempt to support athletes. Through this process, I realised my passion wasn't in athletic development as a whole, but with fighters. I knew their hurdles, their strengths and what motivated them to feel the fear and fight anyway.

Starting Fighters Performance to support the fight community was like setting alight the same fire that burnt to achieve my own accomplishments in the sport. After not making Rio Olympic Games in 2016, I felt extremely lost in life and struggled to find purpose in anything. Now I can say I have worthy direction and feel like I'm back on track chasing my passion.

WHAT MAKES FIGHTERS PERFORMANCE SO UNIQUE?

It's empowering fighters to live and train to their full potential and gain more from the journey that had given me so much.

Fighters Performance is revolutionary. It offers a structured approach to training for amateur and professional fighters. Programming is specific to the individual athletes, leveraging new app-based technologies and takes into account the high demands of combat sport. We hope it will progress traditions, support athletes and coaches from club level, and provide a pathway to success for those who aspire to stand on the podium at the Olympic Games.

HABITS, ROUTINES AND TIPS /

WHAT DOES YOUR MORNING ROUTINE LOOK LIKE?

I write a note to myself every morning that is consistent with my vision for Fighters Performance.

It's written on a post-it note, folded and put in my pocket so when I reach into my pocket during the day and feel that note, it reminds me of my 'why' and motivates me to get those necessary things done.

When I was a competitor I would write out my vision of the Olympic dream on that note as soon as I woke and put it in my pocket. Every time I reached for something in my pocket I would envision myself with the medal around my neck.

It always said, "I'm looking into the audience for my parents from the top of the gold medal podium at the 2016 Olympic Games listening to the national anthem".

WHAT NEW BELIEF, BEHAVIOUR OR HABIT HAS MOST IMPROVED YOUR LIFE?

I'm open and transparent about my ideas. I share my thoughts and encourage others to do the same.

I think out really loud without fear of someone else 'stealing' my idea. As an athlete, I felt the same way with my techniques and what I had learnt. If you are copying someone else you are 10 years behind and I believe I'm forward-thinking.

There is a story about the Russian Judo team where spies discovered by satellite that the team were running in the snow. So all over the world, teams decided that running must be the most important thing in a teams training program. Turns out the Russian team had left the key to the Dojo at home, so the coach made the whole team run back and get it.

WHAT ARE ONE TO THREE BOOKS THAT HAVE GREATLY CHANGED YOUR LIFE?

The 4 Habits of Execution by Chris McChesney, Sean Covey and Jim Huling, *The Alchemist* by Paulo Coelho, *Supertraining* by Yuri Verkhoshansky and Mel Siff

WHEN YOU FEEL UNFOCUSED, HOW DO YOU GET BACK INTO ALIGNMENT?

I take a cold shower, which is also part of my routine. It reminds me that times have been worse and I need to slow down and put things in perspective.

I'm also lucky to be surrounded by people that are in pursuit of their own excellence. I like to talk through things with these people and throw ideas around.

AUSSIE
20
KG

ZADI

Neutral Bay & Surry Hills

SERVICES /

Small Group Training
(Strength/HIIT)
Female Only Studio

POWER AND PASSION • Zadi is not just a gym – it's a fitness concept of HIIT, strength and functional training for badass women. Their philosophy is to 'ignite power and share passion', employing female-specific workouts developed by Sydney-based exercise scientist Damien Kelly – powered with seamless booking systems and cutting-edge bespoke technology to monitor your fitness progress. Smash through workouts such as 'Slay Day', 'Badass Boss' and 'Toned AF' with like-minded women. The metabolic circuit-training methods have been designed specifically for women's bodies, to produce game-changing results. Zadi's vibe feels more nightclub than gym. There's high-energy music, bright lights and a stripped-back warehouse setting, but instead of sipping cocktails, you'll get intense workouts that promise to "unleash the extraordinary" in you.

ZAD

CYCOLOGY CLUB

350 Bourke St, Surry Hills

SERVICES /

Group Spin Classes

RHYTHM RIDING • Cycology Club is an indoor cycle studio and lifestyle space that will see you leave on a natural high. Riding to the beat of the music, in sync with your crew, they revitalise indoor cycling by adding in upper body movement and choreographed weight tracks that strengthen and tone your muscles. Classes are 50 minutes of intense cardio workout. Designed more like a nightclub than a gym, Cycology Club contains state-of-the-art audio visual technology, 35 Schwinn Carbon Blue bikes and a climate-controlled environment for your enjoyment. The studio is situated in the brand new Short Lane development in Surry Hills. Pre or post class, Cycology Club also features the 'M3 room – an area dedicated to mindfulness, mobility and meditation. Full male and female change facilities are also available. The club is a cashless environment.

CYCOLOGYCLUB.COM

INFINITE CYCLE

Bondi Junction, CBD & Waterloo

SERVICES /

Group Spin Classes
(Rhythm, Peloton, Race)

ROAD WORTHY • Infinite Cycle is the only place in Australia and New Zealand where you can ride the incredible RealRyder® indoor bikes, which enable you to burn 20% more calories than a regular indoor cycling class. This is because these bikes can actually 'move' beneath you, making you able to turn, tilt and lean as you ride – the same way as if you were on a road bike. Specialist Infinite Cycle instructors guide riders through an interactive audio-visual experience delivered through high-definition screens. Riders can track their vital statistics from each ride, allowing them to monitor progress and fitness outcomes. Three distinct styles of classes – Peloton, Rhythm and Race – will challenge and keep you evolving to a place where your mind can rest and your body can experience infinite possibilities it never knew existed.

SCENIC CYCLE

CBD & Manly

SERVICES /

Group Spin Classes
Retail

THRILL RIDE • Scenic Cycle is your ticket to experience fitness in a fresh new way. Imagine taking on a spin class in front of two massive screens that project beautiful HD vision from all over the globe, while you pedal away to inspiring sound?

In one class you'll be climbing some of the steepest hills in the French Alps, then sprinting through the tropics of Fiji in another. Then why not attack the rolling hills and Fjords of Norway? All from the safety and comfort of a luxury indoor space with high-quality equipment and technology. There's nothing else like it in the world. Scenic Cycle is a spin experience that is truly unique, motivating and unforgettable. Bringing the great outdoors inside will give you a picture-perfect thrill ride you may not expect.

VICIOUS CYCLE

27 Park St, Sydney

SERVICES /

Group Spin Classes

BREAK THE CYCLE • Vicious Cycle is a Rhythm Riding studio in the Sydney CBD, offering a multi-sensory ride experience with a fine balance of music, movement and motivation. The signature programmed sessions combine a full-body workout that connects your mind and body, making you stronger mentally, physically and emotionally. Led by a team of passionate, experienced instructors who embody the Vicious spirit, the classes will leave you feeling sweaty, energised, stronger and brighter. As part of the community, there are often special events to get involved in, such as weekend 'breakactions' in scenic destinations to recharge and workout. Ride united as part of a collective movement where you learn to 'hold on and let go'. The aim is for you to build great new long-term lifestyle habits and break negative cycles together.

VICIOUSCYCLE.COM.AU

BY JACKIE ALEXANDER / CO-FOUNDER HUMMING PUPPY

MORE THAN A WORKOUT /

Steeped in ancient wisdom, yoga nourishes the needs of mind, body and spirit in a way that resonates deeply for its devotees – the perfect antidote to fast-paced modern life.

I TRULY LOVE SYDNEY. WITH ITS HARBOUR VIEWS, RESTAURANTS AND BEAUTIFUL BEACHES, IT'S THE PERFECT MIX OF WORK AND PLAY.

There's no doubt, however, that living in this beautiful city can be stressful, even for the most relaxed, beach-loving yogi. It's fast-paced. The work hours are often long. Time spent looking at screens is even longer. For many, the majority of their days are spent sitting in chairs, hustling at their desks. This worldly city demands a lot from us – physically, emotionally, spiritually.

So, naturally, the focus on health and wellbeing is widespread. Long gone are the days where Sydneysiders had to travel far and wide to attend yoga classes in studios overflowing with patchouli and international backpackers. Studios are now intentionally designed to welcome and encourage like-minded communities to connect and flourish. Superfood bars seem to be on every corner. Activewear is now acceptable for brunch, lunch and everything in between. Health and wellness isn't a fad. It is here to stay.

I, for one, cannot be more pleased with this shift in culture. The increased curiosity and appreciation for yoga is a testament to the incredible ways in which it transforms lives. As more studies confirm what Eastern philosophy has known for centuries, the power of yoga has transcended its 'hippie stereotype' of the past and has found its place in mainstream culture.

For many, the entry point to yoga is a form of exercise. There is no doubt as to the amazing physical changes the practice has on the body. I find it interesting when people say yoga isn't a hard workout – anyone who has been to a good yoga class can tell you this is not the case. I see yoga as a 'work in', with the 'workout' being a great drawcard to get people in the door; they stay for the impact it has on the mind.

Yoga is much more than physical movements; it's about connection and intimacy with ourselves, to our entire being – mind, body, breath and spirit. The meaning of the Sanskrit word yoga is 'union' and 'connection'. It's this holistic approach to wellbeing that makes this practice truly beautiful.

Every time we walk into the studio, we are taking a stand for our own self-care. We are checking in with ourselves. We are building internal relationships. We are learning compassion – for others and ourselves.

We are stilling the mind, or at least trying to. It doesn't matter how comfortably we can sit in asana (yoga postures) or how flexible we are. All that matters is that we showed up.

We, humans, weren't designed to be 'on' all the time. We weren't created to sit at desks, to meet impending deadlines, yet our culture now demands this of us. Yoga is a way to offload some of that pressure. A place where we can pause and breathe. It gives us space to realign our bodies and to reconnect with our breath.

The side effects of this are plentiful. Less stress, increased flexibility, improved energy and vitality, protection from injury, weight reduction... the list is endless. Yet, perhaps the most important side effect is the deepening of the relationship we have with ourselves. It's why so many Sydneysiders try a class – and why so many keep coming back.

JACKIE ALEXANDER / *Jackie began her career in hospitality, then worked in the dental industry for almost a decade. After a difficult knee reconstruction, she began practising yoga and noticed profound shifts in her energy, body and attitude to life. She soon realised yoga was her path and opened Humming Puppy in 2015. She now has three studios in three locations: Sydney, Melbourne and New York.*

HUMMINGPUPPY.COM

BE ONE YOGA

20 Hargrave St, Darlinghurst

SERVICES /

- Yoga
- Group Classes
- Private Classes
- Teacher Training
- Wellness Packages
- Workshops

COMPLETE CONNECTION • Be One is a boutique yoga studio hidden away in a haven amid the lively hustle of Darlinghurst. The studio aspires to authentically live up to its name by being a place where people from all walks of life come together – to be one with their bodies, minds and hearts, no matter their background, experiences or level of ability. In this space, the team gets bodies moving, transform minds, and inspires individuals to create positive changes in their lives. Class types include vinyasa, hot flow, hatha and yin. Be One's core belief is that when you are connected and 'one' with your heart's truest intention, you live freely – and become free to live a life you choose.

BEONEYOGA.COM.AU

BODYMINDLIFE

Bondi Beach, Kirrawee, Potts Point, Redfern & Surry Hills

SERVICES /

- Yoga
- Pilates
- Group Classes
- Teacher Training
- Events

SWEAT SURRENDER • BodyMindLife is one of Sydney's top yoga and Pilates studios, with five beautiful, light-filled locations in Surry Hills, Potts Point, Bondi Beach, Redfern and Kirrawee. The studio's expert teachers come from around the world and offer more than 450 classes each week – as well as regular events, workshops and teacher trainings – that get students of all levels to sweat, play and surrender. Yoga classes vary from yin to Vinyasa, held in a constant temperature of between 26 and 30 degrees Celsius. Reformer Pilates sessions range from gentle alignment to flow or dynamic, which will get the heart rate up and muscles working. The Surry Hills studio has a far infrared sauna to help soothe aches and pains and detoxify the body.

BODYMINDLIFE.COM

HOT DOG YOGA

1, 15 Knox St, Double Bay

SERVICES /

Yoga
Group Classes
Private Classes
Events

HEAT SEEKERS • Hot Dog Yoga combines playfulness, heat and downward facing dogs with a focus on creative, intelligent sequencing – helping all who enter the studio to connect with themselves through breath and conscious movement. Not to mention connecting with doggy concierge, Pavlova. The studio design channels minimalist chic with Scandinavian style, with floor-to ceiling windows flooding the space with natural light. It also provides all modern amenities, including provided mats, lockers and showers. There's a range of classes to cater to all levels, from beginners to advanced practitioners, as well as different intensities to suit individual preferences. The team has matched these class styles to their optimal temperature for practice. Hot Dog Yoga exists to inspire and empower people to lead mindful, active lives.

HOTDOGYOGA.COM.AU

HUMMING PUPPY

146 Abercrombie St, Redfern

SERVICES /

Yoga
Group Classes
Workshops

GOOD VIBRATIONS • When taking a class at Humming Puppy, one of the first things you will notice is that the room quite literally 'hums'. The yoga space, or 'shala', was engineered by a world-leading acoustic expert to install a combination of frequencies to enhance and deepen your experience. Being immersed in 7.83hz and 40hz helps you to naturally produce matching frequencies through a process of entrainment. Otherwise known as the Schumann Resonance, 7.83hz is actually the frequency of the Earth itself and helps to 'ground' you through your practice. Associated with the gamma brainwave activity, 40hz helps achieve states of peak performance. The signature "hum" that is played in all classes is a recording of Co Founder Jackie playing a himalayan crystal singing bowl that was detuned to 40 hertz and oscillates throughout all classes.

HUMMINGPUPPY.COM

MODERN MOVEMENT

Balgowlah & Mona Vale

SERVICES /

Yoga
Pilates

MEDICINE IN MOVEMENT • The vision for Modern Movement is yoga with purpose – creating an experience that offers more than just a good sweat and moves deeper than just the physical body. Their sessions are steeped in ancient wisdom, tradition and connection but are also an evolution into the modern world of functional movement, psychology, and anatomical biomechanics. Both studios in the Northern Beaches are bright and beautiful, offering styles suited to every body, at any stage of experience, including vinyasa, slow flow, yin yoga and pilates. The signature style is modern vinyasa. Classes are heated, strong, dynamic, and transformational, challenging more than just physical limits. Through the physical flow, you'll find power and un-tap the more subtle parts of your mind and purpose. It's medicine in movement.

MODERNMOVEMENT.COM.AU

ONE HOT YOGA

34 Kellett St, Potts Point

SERVICES /

Yoga
Pilates
Retreats
Workshops

CONSCIOUS CONDITIONING • At One Hot Yoga & Pilates, they focus on a single intention: living well. This translates to practicing the disciplines of yoga and Pilates to elevate the everyday from routine to ritual. Their studios centre on the two elements that compose the human body: water and air. One Hot Yoga incorporates a hydronic heating system into the classes, hydrating the eyes and skin as the temperature increases. The state-of-the-art air filtration system nourishes the body and cleanses the organs with a constant stream of oxygen, which also ensures the rooms remain feeling fresh with a subtle spiciness from their signature scent. The studio features raw and recycled building materials, deluxe showers and a custom Ayurvedic hair and body-care range, to make the process comfortable so you can push your practice further.

ONEHOTYOGA.COM.AU

SKY LAB

342 Elizabeth St, Surry Hills

SERVICES /

- Aerial Fitness
- Aerial Yoga
- Aerial Pilates
- Aerial Barre
- Aerial Meditation
- Apparel & Clothing

AIM HIGH • Ever wondered what it's like to fly? Sure you have. Now you can feel the closest thing to it – in a yoga class. At Skylab Yoga, you'll be suspended in a hammock that will help you get into antigravity positions you wouldn't otherwise be able to achieve. Not only will the hammock assist you in mastering simple inversions and building strength, it will also help refine your alignment. These classes are great if you want to kick your yoga practice up a notch, but they'll also do wonders for compressed joints. There's also no need to worry about complexity – the classes are not as hard as they appear to be. Just be sure to start with a low-intensity session and an open approach to give it ago. You'll fly high in no time.

SPACE STUDIO

400 Barangaroo Ave, Barangaroo

SERVICES /

Yoga
Barre
Meditation
Pilates

MIND AND MOVEMENT • In the heart of Sydney's bustling CBD, The Space Studio offers a sanctuary for its members to calm the mind and strengthen the body. Enter the studio, leave the outside world behind and work on whatever is important to enhance your day; be it finding tranquillity, energy or focus. The bright and airy studio is purpose-built for the practice of yoga, barre, Pilates and meditation – transformed through light projections and soundscapes to inspire the energy of your practice. The Space Studio's philosophy is about 'mind and movement', designed to calm the mind and strengthen the body. Yoga classes include Vinyasa (heated and non-heated), yin, flow and unwind, and meditation. Pilates focuses on matwork and barre uses props for an all-body workout.

 THESPACESTUDIO.COM.AU

W1LL

657 Pacific Hwy, St Leonards

SERVICES /

Yoga
Meditation
Event Space
Wellness Events

BEING ONE • W1LL is the evolution of yoga and meditation: a modern take on an ancient practice. Offering a truly immersive experience, their classes are built around curated playlists and beautiful visuals. Disconnect from the busyness of life as you step into the dimly lit studio, then connect to yourself and your mat with guided and live classes on the large screen. W1LL's uniquely designed sequences deliver a consistent practice, increasing your strength and mobility, improving tone and boosting clarity and productivity. There's a tailored range of practice options suitable for all levels. The 1 in W1LL stands for 'one human'. Every time you connect to the mat or purchase one of their products you're helping a human in need through their foundation, The Human Kind Project.

I WILL CREATE CHANGE

BARRE BODY

Bondi Junction, CBD & Surry Hills

SERVICES /

Barre
Meditation
Pilates
Yin
Yoga

RAISING THE BARRE • With 10 studios across Australia, including Sydney CBD, Surry Hills and Bondi Junction, Barre Body offers an extensive suite of classes for every body, including barre, yoga, Pilates, cardio and yin. The signature Elements class takes its name from the elements necessary for a balanced, effective workout routine. The choreographed session covers the essentials for a one-hour full mind and body workout: 'sweat, sculpt and still'. This means cardio, strengthening and toning, and meditation and mindful movement. A new class is released every eight weeks. Delivered by a team of world-class teachers and set in gorgeous boutique studios, Barre Body will help you tone, transform and love your body, and help to clear your mind. It's an addiction you won't want to kick.

BARREBODY.COM.AU

BARRE BODY

BARRE PROJECT

55 York St, Sydney

SERVICES /

Barre
Cardio Barre
Group Classes
Resistance Training
Private Classes
Yoga

FITNESS FUSION • The Barre Project is a unique, effective, attitude-filled fitness program, fusing barre work with low impact bodyweight exercises and strength and interval training, cardio and principles from Pilates and yoga. Each instructor-led class methodically fatigues the body to create a strong, long and lean sculpted physique while increasing heart health. Added benefits include improved posture, stability and flexibility. The empowering team of instructors believes a workout can benefit the mind, body and soul, while being low impact and sustainable for the body and joints. The Barre Project's athletic, musically driven approach leaves no muscle group unworked, and every class differs, resulting in muscle confusion and undeniable results. They're eager to bring together all age groups and fitness levels to realise their full fitness potential.

THEBARREPROJECT.COM.AU

FLUIDFORM PILATES

1A Danks St, Waterloo

SERVICES /

Equipment Pilates
Barre Attack
Mat Pilates
Pre & Post Natal

FORM AND FUNCTION • Fluidform is an energetic Pilates studio on Danks Street, offering personalised programming that caters to every individual's specific needs. Their posture analysis system has been developed over 10 years working with hundreds of people. Fluidform a variety of classes available, focused on strength and flexibility, including matwork, equipment Pilates, Swiss ball, Barre Attack and HIIT Pilates sessions. The beautiful, expansive studio features high ceilings, a modern fit-out, split mezzanine level, and full length mirrors throughout. As part of its high level of comfort and service, Fluidform provides fresh towels, filtered water, a waiting lounge, bathroom, change room and a climate-controlled environment. Director Kirsten King is passionate about the functional and aesthetic changes that Pilates can provide for each and every body.

KX PILATES

Over 8 Studios in Sydney

SERVICES /

Reformer Pilates
Group Classes
Private Classes

TARGETED TRAINING • KX Pilates is a twist on traditional reformer Pilates, offering a workout that targets the whole body through continuous, precise, controlled movements. Their style of training uses functional exercises that increase intensity while engaging the core and cardiovascular conditioning. Based on the 'isolate, fatigue, stretch' principle, KX Pilates classes get you burning more calories per minute and continuing to burn hours after the class has finished. There's a range of specialised classes available at KX's boutique, well-appointed studios in multiple locations – from pre and post natal, advanced levels and personalised private classes for all levels.

KXPILATES.COM.AU

PEACHES PILATES

Bondi & Maroubra

SERVICES /

Group Training
Mums & Bubs
Personal Training
Pregnancy & Postnatal

WELLNESS REFUGE • The focus of the Peaches method is to change your perception of Pilates – the workouts are fast, fun, and deliver a serious burn. While Pilates is the focus, Peaches offers a variety of classes, all with core strength and spinal health training instilled within. Sweat it out with boxing, weights, barre, yoga and circuit-style sessions with the knowledge that classic technique will keep your lower back safe and your posture on point. The women behind Peaches, Tori and Bec, grew tired of the sterile and image-based theme of fitness, so they've created their own 'wellness refuge' including workshops with holistic insights.

Peaches Pilates has two studio locations in Sydney's beautiful beachside suburbs, Bondi and Maroubra, as well as an online program.

PURE BALANCE STUDIO

407 New South Head Rd, Double Bay

SERVICES /

Clinical and Studio Pilates
Feldenkrais Movement
MIH outpatient-Consulting
Pre-and Post Natal
Rehabilitation
Sport Programming
Weight Loss Training

MIX IT UP • Pure Balance Studio uses a hybrid training system that combines Pilates, cardio and strength. These essential elements create an efficient way to get your heart pumping, to tone up and stay bendy. All sessions utilise the Pilates zone, which has a full range of Balance Body Pilates equipment. Instructors will also take you through your paces in the 'functional training zone', with wall bars, spin, rowing, water training and weights. These special programs are offered to complement the Pure Balance system, which includes weight-loss training, clinical and studio Pilates, pre- and post-natal Pilates, Feldenkrais movement, rehabilitation, sport science programming and outdoor training. You can choose to mix multiple workouts into one session or just keep it pure with Pilates only.

PUREBALANCESTUDIO.COM.AU

VIVE ACTIVE

145 Old Pittwater Rd, Brookvale

SERVICES /

Reformer Pilates
Group Classes
Private Classes
Private Group

TRAIN AND TRANSFORM • Drawing on 100 years of exercise physiology, Vive Active transforms Pilates into a complete sensory experience, using state-of-the-art lighting, sound and design. Their mission is to be a catalyst for change – to feed your hunger for results, strength, fun, connection, energy and longevity, with strength, flexibility and endurance at its core. Vive has united some of the nation's most engaging and highly skilled trainers, committed to helping you find your greatness. Let them be your guides on the journey, and use the studio as your destination for growth. All ages and all walks of life are welcome to be part of the community with a shared ambition: to transcend your here and now, to better your best.

[PARAMOUNT RECREATION CLUB · SURRY HILLS]

MARTIAL ARTS & BOXING /

There's a wealth of academies and gyms available for Sydney's fight enthusiasts, covering a range of styles, levels and techniques in the world of martial arts. Boxers aren't forgotten either, with many specialists sparring around the city. There's also classes for both kids and adults in Brazilian Jiu-Jitsu and Thai kickoxing, plus female-only sessions.

12 ROUNDS FITNESS
Alexandria, Bondi Junction, Brookvale & Mascot

8 LIMBS
38/40 Bronte Rd, Bondi Junction

BIKINI BODS
4/42-46 Wattle Rd, Brookvale

BONDI BOXING GYM
284 Bondi Rd, Bondi

BOXING WORKS
Glebe, Kings Cross & Surry Hills

CORPORATE FIGHT CENTRE
36-38 Wentworth Ave, Surry Hills

FIGHTERS PERFORMANCE
78-80 George St, Redfern

FIT1
96 Newcastle St, Rose Bay

LEGACY BRAZILIAN JIU JITSU
36-42 Chippen St, Sydney

ROOTS BRAZILIAN JIU JITSU
CBD, Botany, Brookvale, Erskinville & Hurstville

SYDNEY JIU JITSU ACADEMY
17 Carter Rd, Brookvale

VT1 MARTIAL ARTS ACADEMY
390 Eastern Valley Way, Chatswood

VAULT BOXING & FITNESS
26 Queen St, Chippendale

XAVIER JIUJITSU
171 William St, Darlinghurst

[PARAMOUNT RECREATION CLUB - SURRY HILLS]

OUTDOOR SPACES /

Sydney is blessed with natural beauty and plenty of green spaces to train. From parks and reserves, to scenic lookouts and beaches, you'll find many motivating places for exercise and fun in the sun.

BICENTENNIAL PARK
Glebe

BONDI PARK
Bondi Beach

BURROWS PARK
Clovelly

CAMPERDOWN PARK
Camperdown

CHRISTISON PARK
Vaucluse

DUDLEY PAGE RESERVE
Dover Heights

FRENCHMANS BAY
Frenchmans Bay

LEICHHARDT PARK
Lilyfield

MAROUBRA BEACH
Maroubra

MA'ANSHAN PARK
Hurstville

MOORE RESERVE
Hurstville Grove

OBSERVATORY HILL PARK
Millers Point

PRINCE ALFRED PARK
Surry Hills

QUEENS PARK
Queens Park

ROTARY PARK
Riverwood

RUSHCUTTERS BAY PARK
Rushcutters Bay

SYDNEY PARK
Alexandria

WENTWORTH PARK
Ultimo

[SELPH HEALTH STUDIOS · ROSEBERY]

BODY
MIND
SOUL

SPAS. MASSAGE. MEDITATION
FLOAT TANKS. CRYOTHERAPY
MINDFUL & WELLNESS SPACES

CHI, THE SPA

176 Cumberland St, Sydney

SERVICES /

Body Treatments
Facials
Massage
Pool

PEACE AND PRIVACY • Drawing inspiration from the legendary Shangri-La – a place of personal peace, enchantment and wellbeing – Chi, The Spa is truly relaxing and private. Each suite is independent and exclusive to you, including its own pool. The decor is minimalistic and clean with lowlights and open space, creating a unique Thai ambience and a distinctive impression of peace and stability.

While massages and other treatments are based on traditional Asian wellness practices, there's also Australian healing techniques using botanical ingredients from the region. Don't worry if it's your first visit – one of Chi's consultants will talk with you to ensure the best treatment for your needs. Be sure to inform them of any pain areas to avoid – it's all about you and your enjoyment.

氣
Chi

THE DARLING SPA

80 Pyrmont St, Pyrmont

SERVICES /

Facials
Massage
Natural Therapies

PURE INDULGENCE • The Darling Spa is one of the finest and most luxurious spas in Sydney, offering a comprehensive range of face and body treatments to leave you relaxed and refreshed from head to toe. From facials, massages and body wraps, to dedicated treatments for men and pregnant women, the spa is an inner-city haven for pure indulgence and rejuvenation. The centre, located on the second level of The Darling hotel, features 11 treatment rooms, two exclusive couples suites, a Moroccan Hammam chamber, steam room, Jacuzzi, fitness centre and Kinesis wall. There are several custom experiences available, depending on your needs, such as the 'Darling De-stress' and 'Total Body and Soul'. The Darling Spa uses international skin care brands La Prairie and ESPA.

THEDARLING.COM.AU

GILLIAN ADAMS SPA

1356 Pacific Hwy, Turramurra

SERVICES /

Beauty
Facials
Massage
Pool
Spa

EXUDE BEAUTY • Gillian Adams Salon & Spa opened 30 years ago as a groundbreaking urban oasis centred on wellbeing. Providing services for hair, beauty, body and cuisine all in one place, the salon's purpose is to help guests find their inner beauty and let it glow from the inside out. Their signature Urban Spa experience revives the tradition of ancient pools and begins with time the Aquamedic Pool, with needle point and massage jets to tone skin and promote blood circulation for full relaxation. Then to the steam room for an intensified aromatherapy experience. Relax in a lounge with juice, tea, coffee and fruit while waiting for treatments. There's also a garden to enjoy a nutritious breakfast, lunch or high tea with complimentary wines. Anti-ageing treatments are available by appointment in the VIP suite.

THE DAY SPA BY CHUAN

89-113 Kent St, Sydney

SERVICES /

Facials
Gymnasium
Massage Therapy
Pool
Spa

UNDERGROUND RETREAT • At Langham Hotel's Day Spa by Chuan, it's all about four words: detox, renew, relax and rejuvenate. The Day Spa is a lavish and serene underground sanctuary with a focus on providing a holistic experience for all guests. As soon as you enter the peaceful space you'll begin to feel at ease. There's a range of healing therapies to treat the mind as well as the body, performed by highly qualified therapists using exclusive German Babor products. A range of innovative new treatments will aid in complete indulgence and pampering, including spa and cosmetic facials, massages, stone therapy and scrubs. Packages are on offer for busy corporates, ladies days, couples and bride and groom preparation.

THE SPA AT THE HYATT

7 Hickson Rd, The Rocks

SERVICES /

Holistic Treatments
Gymnasium
Steam Room
Rooftop Pool

INNER-CITY SANCTUARY • Let The Spa at Park Hyatt become your personal haven in the heart of Sydney, as you indulge in peace, quiet and replenishing luxury. The Spa's team of specialists use a range of holistic treatments to leaving you feeling enriched and renewed, including massage, facials, body wraps and exfoliation. Invigorating natural ingredients, such as melaleuca, myrtle, Australian sea kelp, native hibiscus and lavender, will rejuvenate your senses. In addition to soothing experiences, the luxury spa also includes a fully equipped gymnasium, relaxation room, aromatherapy steam rooms, and a rooftop pool and terrace available exclusively to spa members and residing guests. Treat yourself to complete tranquility as you experience the ultimate spa experience at The Spa.

HYATT.COM

SOL SPA

2 Laguna St, Vaucluse

SERVICES /

Body Scrubs
Facials
Therapies
Manicure
Pedicure
Massage

CLOSE TO NATURE • Inspired by wellness, nature and health, Sol Spa is a blissful escape from everyday life, situated in the heart of the eastern suburbs. On arrival, you'll be greeted by a team of wellness specialists and guided through your facial, massage or holistic consultation to ensure you will have an exceptional, customised experience. Wander through the lush gardens and then enter the spa, where you'll be greeted by the scent of lemongrass and a fresh range of herbal water infusions and organic tastings. Inside, you'll be surrounded by ancient relics, luscious plants and comforting throws to calm and re-energise your mind. Sol Spa's range of heavenly spa treatments, including massage, facials and acupressure, feature aromatic oils, spices and herbs, with a focus on natural and botanical ingredients.

SPAQ

49 Market St, Sydney

SERVICES /

Barber Shop
Body Exfoliation
Facial Therapy
Foot Therapy
Hair Treatment
Massage Therapy
Social Spa-ing
Steam Room

DESIGNER DECADENCE • Discover a touch of old-world glamour at concept spa, spaQ. Sophistication and relaxation is infused into the entire experience, from the uniforms and menu options to the philosophy of indulgence. The design cleverly uses colour and quirky features to mirror the heritage of QT Sydney's CBD location, above two of the city's most historical buildings. Rather than insisting on pre-selection of treatments, spaQ encourages you to book a block of time and make a treatment selection on the day, using the therapist's knowledge to help guide you to the perfect choice. Facilities include six treatment rooms, a barber, a steam room with ice fountain, full-amenity changerooms, a relaxation lounge and spa boutique. The treatment menu includes massages, facials and body treatments by USpa and Skeydor.

MELISSA AMBROSINI /

Melissa Ambrosini is a speaker, self-love teacher, bestselling author of Mastering Your Mean Girl and Open Wide, and host of the top-rated podcast, The Melissa Ambrosini Show. In her signature straight-talking style, Melissa teaches women how to unlock their full potential, master their inner Mean Girl, smash through limiting beliefs, and ditch the self-doubt so they can start living the life of their dreams.

HOW HAS YOUR LIFE EXPERIENCE INSPIRED YOU TO PAVE YOUR PATH INTO A SUCCESSFUL BUSINESS?

It all began back in 2010. I hit rock bottom and ended up in hospital after burning the candle at both ends. Before that, I was a professional dancer, actress and TV presenter. Although that may sound really glamorous — and although it may have looked like I had a great life on the outside — on the inside, I was dying. My health was plummeting, my relationships were toxic, I no longer liked the work I was doing, plus I was dealing with anxiety, panic attacks, depression and an eating disorder. When I ended up in hospital it was a huge wake-up call for me, and that's what sparked me to turn my whole life around and led me to my true path.

From there, I wanted to get happy and healthy again, so I made that my mission. I went on to study holistic nutrition and health and life coaching and became a qualified yoga teacher. I learned how to meditate and studied AcuEnergetics (energy healing work). But most important of all, I began my inward journey to uncover the true me.

From there, I started sharing what I was learning on this newfangled thing (that none of my family or friends had heard of) called a 'blog'. I began sharing my lessons and learnings on my blog, in my ebooks, online courses and talks. I knew I was onto something because women were coming up to me in the street and saying: "Thank you so much for your honesty, I thought I was the only one who dealt with eating issues and a lack of self-love." Since 2010 I have stayed on my path and true to my mission, which is to inspire women to unlock their full potential and live the life of their dreams. Everything I do and create is with that intention in my mind and heart.

WHAT SPECIFIC STRATEGIES DO YOU OR HAVE YOU USED TO OVERCOME LIMITING BELIEFS?

I practice my *Mastering Your Mean Girl* three-step process to overcome all my limiting beliefs. It goes like this:

1. Practice awareness. Become aware of when your inner Mean Girl pops up and tells you that you're not good enough, thin enough, smart enough, whatever enough. Most times we are so unconscious and not present that we aren't even aware of her internal dialogue, so bringing your awareness to her words is the first step.

2. Gently close the door on her. Once you are aware that she has popped up, you can now choose to gently close the door on her. It's not about fighting her, or waging an inner battle — that'll just cause more pain and suffering. Instead, it's a graceful act that comes from a place of love.

3. Choose love instead. Once you have gently closed the door on her, choose to come back to your heart and choose love instead of fear. It's so much more fulfilling when you do.

WHAT'S THE SOURCE OF YOUR DRIVE TO EMPOWER OTHERS?

God, love, the Universe, a higher purpose (whatever you want to call it), that's what drives me. We are here on Earth to serve others. It's our purpose and mission.

TACTICS, ROUTINES AND HABITS /

WHAT DOES THE FIRST HOUR OF YOUR MORNING ROUTINE LOOK LIKE?

My day always starts with gratitude in bed with my husband. Then, if we have time we will connect, which is always my favourite way to start the day. After that I head to the bathroom to scrape my tongue (which is an ancient Ayurvedic ritual), I'll then wash my face, brush my teeth and do coconut oil pulling (which is another ancient Ayurvedic ritual I love). After that I meditate for 20 minutes, then do 15 minutes of yoga on my bedroom floor in my PJs. Then I will make myself a delicious hydrating green smoothie and either have a bath with Epsom salts and essential oils or a shower followed by a self-love essential oils massage. Then I start my day.

WHAT IS THE BEST OR MOST WORTHWHILE INVESTMENT YOU'VE EVER MADE?

The investment in myself. Getting coaches for business, health, life and spiritual mentors has been the best investment I have ever made. We all need coaches and every cent I have spent has been well worth it.

WHAT NEW BELIEF, BEHAVIOUR OR HABIT HAS MOST IMPROVED YOUR LIFE?

Learning how to master my inner Mean Girl has changed my life! It's a very simple process, but you need to practice it daily. We have between 60,000 and 80,000 thoughts per day, so at the start, you may need to master her 80,000 times. But, like anything, the more you practice, the better and better you get at it.

WHAT IS YOUR BEST WELLNESS TIP FOR FEELING GOOD?

Start meditating daily. It's life-changing and one of the best things you can do for your health and happiness. My guided meditations are a great place to start.

THE INDIGO PROJECT

33 Foster St, Surry Hills

SERVICES /

Mental Health
Psychology
Counselling
Coaching
Courses
Special Events
Workshops

PROGRESSIVE AND PROACTIVE • The Indigo Project is a different kind of psychology practice – their mission is to 'help you get your sh*t together'. With a team of professional, experienced and friendly psychologists who have been there, they know what you're going through, and how to help you through it. Their therapeutic approach is proactive and designed to empower, with a toolkit derived from fields such as positive psychology, neuroscience and mindfulness. The team specialises in stress, anxiety and relationship issues, helping you get in the right mindset to level up and get to where you want to be.
The Indigo Project is based in a converted warehouse in Surry Hills and their values include compassion, determination, respect, balance and integrity.

CULTIVATE RECOVERY

155 Little Oxford St, Darlinghurst

SERVICES /

Infrared Saunas
NormaTec Compression
Localised Cryo Therapy
Hyperbaric Chamber

REACH YOUR PEAK • Cultivate Recovery is a hidden oasis in the heart of Darlinghurst. Their aim is to help you optimise your lifestyle and physical performance, manage pain, and relieve stress and fatigue. The Cultivate experience provides a high-end service based around a commitment to health and wellbeing. Services include access to infrared saunas, hyperbaric oxygen therapy, targeted cryotherapy treatment and Sydney's first NormaTec lounge - a rapid recovery massage system used by elite athletes and trainers.
The centre provides you with a weekly opportunity to take your training and lifestyle further, bridging the gap between fitness, rest and recovery.

CULTIVATERECOVERY.COM.AU

FLOW REVIVE

50 Oxford St, Paddington

SERVICES /

Float Therapy
Infrared Sauna
NormaTec

SANCTUARY OF STILLNESS • The Flow Revive philosophy is about a balanced and well-rounded lifestyle: one that incorporates movement and exercise, food as medicine, healthy relationships and social interaction. They believe in the importance of having space and time to process life's activities, stresses and excitements, and aims to provides that as a 'sanctuary of stillness'. It's a place where you can recover, cultivate stillness and slow down the nervous system — all of which affects the others aspects of your life. Flow Revive offers float therapy, infrared saunas and NormaTec pulse technology to cover a gamut of specialised treatments that let your body and mind relax, unwind and recover — very much needed in today's fast-paced, high-activity world. They strive to provide ways for you to feel calm and productive, in a friendly and peaceful environment.

FLOWREVIVE.COM.AU

FRESHWATER MASSAGE

55 Harbord Rd, Freshwater

SERVICES /

Massage
Acupuncture
Dry Needling
Meditation
Reiki

PAIN-RELIEF EXPERTISE • Launching in 2013, Freshwater Massage has since broadened its services into a wellness centre with a range of expertise in pain management. Massages are based on a variety of soft tissue techniques to help prolong the effects of relief and keep you on track – ideal for active professionals suffering from short and long term pain. Treatment techniques include remedial, Bowen, trigger point and myofascial release, with clinical practitioners applying the right combination for your pain, to provide fast and lasting results. With a background in corrective exercise and personal experience with pain management, the team can help with pain and tension caused through injuries, postural misalignments or leading a sedentary lifestyle. The beautiful wellness centre is based in a former art gallery and continues this tradition by exhibiting the work of local artists.

FRESHWATERMASSAGE.COM.AU

NIMBUS & CO

97 Bondi Rd, Bondi Beach

SERVICES /

Acupuncture
Infrared Sauna
Massage
Naturopathy

DEEPER DETOX • Nimbus & Co is an infrared sauna studio and contemporary wellness space for people to let go, disconnect from the outside world and take time out to nourish their bodies and minds. They have three studios located in Bondi Beach, Byron Bay and Melbourne, with each studio offering a range of modalities and wellness services including private infrared saunas sessions, acupuncture, naturopathy, massage, events and more. The studios use heating panels that allow a deep detox by penetrating the muscles, tissues and cells. The drier air makes it easier to breathe than traditional saunas. Nimbus & Co is a place to fill back up with the mission to 'restore, relax, sweat, meditate'. You will leave feeling restored, harmonious and connected to yourself.

NIMBUSCO.COM.AU

PH CLINIC

48 Sydney Rd, Manly

SERVICES /

Colonic Hydrotherapy
Energetic Healing
Infrared Sauna
Kinesiology
Massage
Naturopathy
Nutrition

HOLISTIC CLINIC • Progressive Health (pH) Clinic is a one-stop holistic health centre in the heart of Manly on Sydney's Northern Beaches. Since 2015, their community of like-minded practitioners has supported thousands of people on their health journey – from elite athletes to terminally ill patients and everyone in between.
What sets pH apart is that the team draws on personal experiences with ill health and recovery to help their clients with understanding and empathy as they journey towards optimal health. The clinic offer a range of alternative therapies to support the body in its healing and honour the mind-body connection, based on a philosophy of continual self betterment.

KOA RECOVERY

143 Botany Rd, Waterloo

SERVICES /

Cryotherapy
Electrical Muscle-Stiulation
Float Therapy
Infrared Sauna
NormaTec

OUTSIDE THE BOX • Koa Recovery is a purpose-built wellness centre specialising in sports recovery and injury management, driven by passion, knowledge and experience. Are you tired and stressed? Looking to improve your performance? Suffering chronic pain? Koa's evidence-based treatments offer a range of benefits to both your physical and mental self. Whether you're a busy mum, elite athlete, weekend warrior, business person or recovering from an injury, there's a service to suit your needs. The centre offers solutions that naturally optimise your body's ability to heal itself, featuring a range of premium therapies such as whole body cryotherapy, float therapy, infrared sauna, NormaTec compression therapy and Compex electro-stimulation. Koa Recovery uses cutting-edge technology and pride themselves on thinking differently, so you can move beyond your limits.

KOARECOVERY.COM.AU

BY JONNI POLLARD / FOUNDER 1 GIANT MIND

HOW TO MAKE MEDITATION A DAILY HABIT /

Despite good intentions, it can seem hard to know where to start with the practice of meditation. But with the right tools, the path to this healthy new habit is easier than you think.

A LOT OF WHAT WE DO ON A DAILY BASIS IS DUE TO HABIT. THESE LEARNT BEHAVIOURS, WHETHER GOOD FOR US OR NOT, HAVE BEEN ESTABLISHED THROUGH REPETITION. INTERESTINGLY ENOUGH, MOST OF OUR HABITS HAVE BEEN FORMED SUBCONSCIOUSLY.

One of the great challenges we face in changing habits and making new ones is overcoming subconscious tendencies. What do we mean by this? It is understood that 90-95% of our thinking is subconscious. Even though we're not aware of these thoughts, they are always influencing our conscious mind and behaviour. This is why changing habits influenced by the subconscious can be difficult.

Meditation is arguably the best new habit to form, as it gives us greater cognitive power to identify and change our subconscious tendencies. Think of meditation as the 'new habit enhancer and old habit breaker'. People who meditate regularly often report finding it much easier to change these patterns. They also notice a huge range of other benefits, such as feeling more present, less stressed and more enthusiastic about meeting life's challenges with greater confidence.

If you are struggling to change old habits or are finding it difficult to establish new ones, the best thing you can do is start a daily meditation practice and see how much easier it is to make the changes in your life you truly desire.

Here are seven simple tips to help make meditation stick as a healthy new daily habit.

1. DOWNLOAD AN APP

Learning to meditate has never been easier or more convenient. At 1 Giant Mind, we have created a free 12-step Learn Meditation course that will teach how to practice a powerful technique that causes deep rest and recovery from stress and fatigue.

The app is packed with great features to support you including a 30-day challenge to help make your practice stick. It's available on iPhone and android.

2. MAKE PRACTICE A PRIORITY

Treat meditation as your most important meeting of the day. Use the app's 'Set a Reminder' tool and put it in your calendar, as a non-negotiable meeting that can't be moved. This one meeting is going to set you up for the rest of the day, giving you greater energy, clarity and resilience to meet any challenge or demand life throws at you.

3. BUDDY UP

Invite one or more friends and family to join you in taking the course and trying the challenge. Teaming up with others is a powerful way to ensure you are held accountable to sticking to your goal.

4. SEE YOUR GOAL AS ACHIEVABLE

If you set aside 15 minutes of the 24 hours you have each day, form a meditation habit equates to only 1% of your total daily activities. When you think of it this way, meditation is very achievable. Investing 1% of your day to improve the remaining 99% with greater energy, clarity and present-moment awareness makes a lot of sense.

5. BE CLEAR ABOUT YOUR 'WHY'

It's very important to know why you are meditating, so you can understand the changes you want to see. The app has a 'Journal' tool where you can make a list and monitor your progress, which is a great way to reinforce the benefits of your practice and keep you motivated.

6. SAVOUR THE BENEFITS

When you begin to notice improvements from meditating regularly, such as feeling more calm and rested or more focused and clear during the day, stop and really savour the moment. Acknowledge these changes have come from your daily meditation practice and the positive impact it's having on your life.

7. DON'T BEAT YOURSELF UP IF YOU MISS A DAY OR TWO

There is no evidence to suggest beating yourself up about anything helps in any way. Negative self-talk isn't going to help you establish a new habit, nor break an old one. When you notice you are trying to talk yourself out of meditating, or self-criticising for not doing it, just smile to yourself and remember that establishing a new habit takes time and repetition and you are well on your way.

JONNI POLLARD /

Jonni Pollard is the co-founder and creator of 1 Giant Mind. An internationally recognised meditation and wisdom teacher, he has dedicated his life to sharing ancient knowledge gained from some of the greatest living masters of our time. He specialises in teaching the art of embodying our true nature to live the most meaningful life possible.

JONNIPOLLARD.COM

SELPH HEALTH STUDIOS

2H Hayes Rd, Rosebery

SERVICES /

Acupuncture
Chiropractic
Massage
Meditation
Nutritionist
Physiotherapy
Pilates
Yoga

BACK IN BALANCE • Selph Health Studios is a holistic wellness studio located in The Cannery, Rosebery. Selph houses a group of specialised health practitioners, as well as a boutique yoga and meditation studio, to help you achieve a mind and body balance. This includes a chiropractor (co-founder Dr Evan Sgammotta), physiotherapist, acupuncturist, remedial masseuse and nutritionist. At Selph, practitioners believe the body must be considered and treated together with the emotional and stress-prone mind. Selph offers specialists in each of the four pillars of health: structural, emotional, nutritional and movement. The specialist team works collaboratively to help you achieve a greater sense of balance, understanding and knowledge of healthy and sustainable habits, and how to maintain them long term.

SELPH.COM.AU

selph

selph
health studios
selph.com.au

THE SHELTER

3 Goldman Ln, Double Bay

SERVICES /

Spin
Boxing
Infared Sauna
Ice Bath

REJUVENATE AND RECOVER • Shelter aims to inspire a healthy community by connecting them with the best in wellness. With a focus on rhythm and music, their high-intensity Ride classes are created to push boundaries without taking the fun out of training. Shelter's infrared and traditional saunas will loosen up stiff or tight muscles, reduce joint pain and give you some much-needed time to yourself. Benefits also include better sleep, improved circulation and detoxification. Aid recovery in a freshwater ice bath, designed to evoke the Japanese practice of soaking to cleanse and recover. There's also a nourishing juicery offering a range of smoothies and supplements. Designed by Anna Trefely, Shelter's sophisticated, minimal space was created with a connection to the eastern beaches of Australia, with each visit intended to be an uplifting sensual experience.

2
1
10
11
19
20
28
29

STRETCH STUDIO

Double Bay, Neutral Bay & Toorak

SERVICES /

One-on-One Professional Assisted Stretching

MUSCLE MEMORIES • It's time to get flexible. Stretch Studios expands the boundaries of health and wellness through a personalised flexibility training session, with a professional "flexologist" trained in the art of stretching. These one-on-one assisted sessions will open up your body, helping you to move better, improve your athletic performance and reduce your risk of injury. Stretching also enhances your posture, coordination, circulation and energy levels. After a good stretch you'll feel instantly improved – every person and set of muscles can benefit. Stretch Studios caters to all body types, but is particularly useful for people who are stiff and want to increase their flexibility safely and efficiently, such as office workers, gym junkies and the elderly. A session will get your blood flowing, leaving you feeling relaxed and released.

KEIRAN BARRY /

Keiran Barry has more than 25 years' experience in the fitness industry. He has trained hundreds of people of all ages and fitness levels, from total novices through to professional athletes in a variety of sports. He's coached at both the Commonwealth and Olympic Games, and has owned and run gyms and corporate fitness businesses and written numerous articles. Keiran's vast experience informs a deep understanding of human physiology and what each individual needs to feel their best.

WHAT IS THE WELL AND WHAT DOES IT REPRESENT?

The Well is a multifaceted wellness centre, with an emphasis on preventative treatment. We promote food and exercise as medicine and see our role as a 'health concierge', in that we identify the issues that prevent you being at your best and offer solutions to those issues. We do it as much as possible under one roof, so all your trainers and therapists are communicating and working together, with your health as their common goal.

TELL US ABOUT YOUR LIFE JOURNEY AND HOW THIS INSPIRED YOUR BUSINESS.

I graduated from uni in 1991 with a degree in Exercise Science and have been in the fitness industry since. I've witnessed it evolve and have seen a lot of trends – some great, some terrible. People are now training like elite athletes, but this needs to be balanced. Elite performance is about staying free of injury and illness and also requires a lot of support from a coach, physical therapist, nutritionist, psychologist and more.

We wanted to create a place where all clients can be treated with a high level of care – the most important principle is to push boundaries but avoid injuries. I strongly believe in the value of traditional training methods mixed with the latest training developments, in a sensible progression. This is the best way to get results. Health comes from within, so we place a lot of value on nutrition and mental fitness.

WHAT DO YOU ENJOY MOST ABOUT RUNNING A HEALTH AND WELLNESS BUSINESS, AND WHAT HAS BEEN THE BIGGEST CHALLENGE?

Although The Well is a small business, there are a lot of elements. I'm part of a team of great people with common goals and a passion for helping others become healthier. The biggest challenge for us is trying to keep focused on our individual roles and strengths, so we don't spread ourselves too thin.

WHICH MOMENTS WILL YOU CHERISH THE MOST, FROM THE MOMENT YOU OPENED UNTIL NOW?

Seeing people make big changes in their life and starting to realise how good they can feel. Seeing a woman with serious chronic pain, drop her daily pain rating from an 8 or 9, to a 3 after just a couple of treatments with some of our therapists and some simple changes to her diet and exercise.

WHAT ARE YOUR PREDICTIONS FOR THE FUTURE OF HEALTH AND WELLNESS?

We we are clearly moving toward an appreciation of overall health and hopefully starting to recognise exercise and food as medicine. I think, in time, the government and health funds will acknowledge the value of integrative health and preventative medicine and start to direct more funding towards keeping people well, rather than just fighting illness. It makes so much sense economically and socially, but as there are a lot of vested interests in keeping the current treatment model, that change is being met with a lot of resistance and will take a long time.

HABITS, ROUTINES AND TIPS /

WHAT IS YOUR DAILY FITNESS AND NUTRITION REGIME?

I don't have a strict daily regime but there are things that are very important to me. I believe in the importance of movement, so I make sure I do strength training, Pilates or something physical every day. Even just 10 minutes of stretch or the foam roller before bed makes a big difference. I love surfing for both the physical joy and mental release and make sure I get in the ocean at least a couple of times each week. I also make sure I meditate each day and spend quality time with my family.

I eat meat but have a predominantly plant based diet, with a big variety of foods for optimal gut health. I drink a lot of water and not much else, with the very occasional beer or vodka on the weekend, and also take a multi-vitamin and mineral each day plus magnesium.

WHICH BOOK (OR BOOKS) HAVE YOU GIVEN AS A GIFT, AND WHY?

This is a really tough question because there is so many choose to from, but my favourite gift book is *A Voyage for Madmen* by Peter Nichols. It covers the first yacht race to single-handedly circumnavigate the globe nonstop in 1968, telling the story of each of the nine sailors who entered and the amazing challenges they faced in an era before GPS. They were out of radio contact for weeks at a time and had to rely totally on themselves. I find it a really challenging and motivating read that highlights human endurance and ingenuity but also shows the frailty of people and the problems with getting literally out of your depth.

WHAT NEW BELIEF, BEHAVIOUR, OR HABIT HAS MOST IMPROVED YOUR LIFE?

I started meditating at a really stressful time in my life and found it has helped me focus on the important things, and kept me calmer and just a little more balanced when life does get stressed. I've still got a long way to go and a lot to learn but feel I'm going in the right direction.

WHAT IS YOUR BEST TIP FOR FEELING GOOD?

Stick to the simple things. Eat mostly healthy foods; schedule time for exercise and relaxation every day. Don't try and please everyone – stay true to yourself and what you believe.

PUNCH.
PUNCH.

THE WELL BONDI

78 Campbell Pde, Bondi Beach

SERVICES /

Acupuncture
Gymnasium
Massage
Naturopathy
Nutrition
Osteopathy
Physiologists
Physiotherapy

PREVENTION PHILOSOPHY • The Well is so much more than just a gym and cafe. It integrates four core pathways that lead to total wellbeing: move, eat, be and feel well. The Well's approach is to create a 'living philosophy' built around a classic idea: prevention is better than cure. Backed by decades of experience and knowledge, the team designs personal health and wellbeing programs that are truly customised to you. This include a broad range of activities and therapies, managed with professional oversight. Each professional at The Well applies authentic care and support to consider your unique needs and preferences – understanding that you need to be engaged and motivated to experience the shared goal of waking up feeling your best every day.

THEWELLBONDI.COM.AU

TO WONDERLAND

71 Glenayr Ave, North Bondi

SERVICES /

Colon Hydrotherapy
Energetic Healing
Facials
Iridology
Massage
Naturopathy
Nutrition
Reflexology
Spa Therapy

WELLNESS WHISPERERS • At To Wonderland, transformation is truly possible, as 'wellness alchemy' works its magic to cleanse, detoxify, rejuvenate and restore. Rather than be limited by chronological age, you will be able to rediscover youthful health, vitality, spirit and glow with a range of energising treatments and a powerful wellness protocol. The treatments are designed to promote longevity and restore balance to body and mind, inspiring rejuvenation of spirit while alleviating stress and fatigue. Each element of the To Wonderland experience activates your original radiant state and ignites your innate healing ability, by way of detoxifying treatments, rejuvenating natural products and bespoke cleanses designed to reawaken your vibrant joy and vitality. Step out of the fast-paced world and into a wellness haven discreetly located by Bondi Beach.

TOWONDERLAND.COM

CRYO

Edgecliff & Rosebery

SERVICES /

Cryotherapy
Cryoslim
Cryo LED

SWIFT RECOVERY • Following years of extensive research, CRYO is the first in Sydney to offer whole body LED light therapy and cryotherapy along with Cryoslim, their unique, three-phase fat reduction treatment. CRYO offers a range of premium services targeting recovery, pain relief, fat loss, anti-ageing and general wellness, at stylish locations in Edgecliff and Rosebery. They have sourced and installed the technologically advanced equipment for optimum safety. The cryotherapy machine ensures overall cold distribution, as the mist moves around your body. Cryoslim is the centre's revolutionary treatment, which uses proven fat-reducing technologies for maximised results. With highly trained staff and a commitment to the health and safety of each of their clients, CRYO is your one-stop shop for health, wellness and anti-ageing.

226
Cryoslim°
Weight loss
The natural way
to lose weight fast
cryo°
cryo°
www.cryo.com.au
1300 33 2796

CORE CRYOTHERAPY

563 Pittwater Rd, Brookvale

SERVICES /

Cryotherapy

COLD COMFORT • A new-age version of the ice bath, whole-body cryotherapy is a high-tech alternative for relieving chronic pain, muscle soreness and inflammation, through exposure to sub-zero dry air for two to three minutes. Core Cryotherapy is a specialist studio that offers this innovative treatment. They operate inside Premier Health and Fitness Gym, the home of the Manly Sea Eagles. Owner and operator Katherine Cole is driven by a passion for body hacking, cellular health and healing the body through natural solutions. She explored these concepts and treatments as part of her own journey to recovery from cancer and other health issues. Through ice therapy, Katherine has helped many people with sports recovery and performance, and assisted others in reducing inflammation and pain, improving skin conditions, losing weight and generally feeling great.

CORECRYOTHERAPY.COM.AU

POLAR BARE CLUB

368 Oxford St, Bondi Junction

SERVICES /

Cryotherapy

COOL CURE • Polar Bare Club Cryo is a warm space for cold blasts that take your health and wellbeing to the next level. Cryotherapy – Greek for 'cold' and 'cure' – is scientifically proven to reduce inflammation in the body, which means tighter skin, pain-free muscles and the best sleep of your life. A session at Polar Bare Club involves stepping into a Cryosauna, in protective clothing, and being sprayed from the neck down by a cold mist of -150 degrees Celsius. This lasts for 90 seconds to three minutes. If you're struggling with muscle aches, pains, strains, tension, aging skin, bloating, fatigue, headaches, insomnia, eczema and more, Cryotherapy can help. Like putting ice on an injury, cold therapy is one of the fastest ways to reduce inflammation and recover.

POLARBARECLUBCRYO.COM.AU

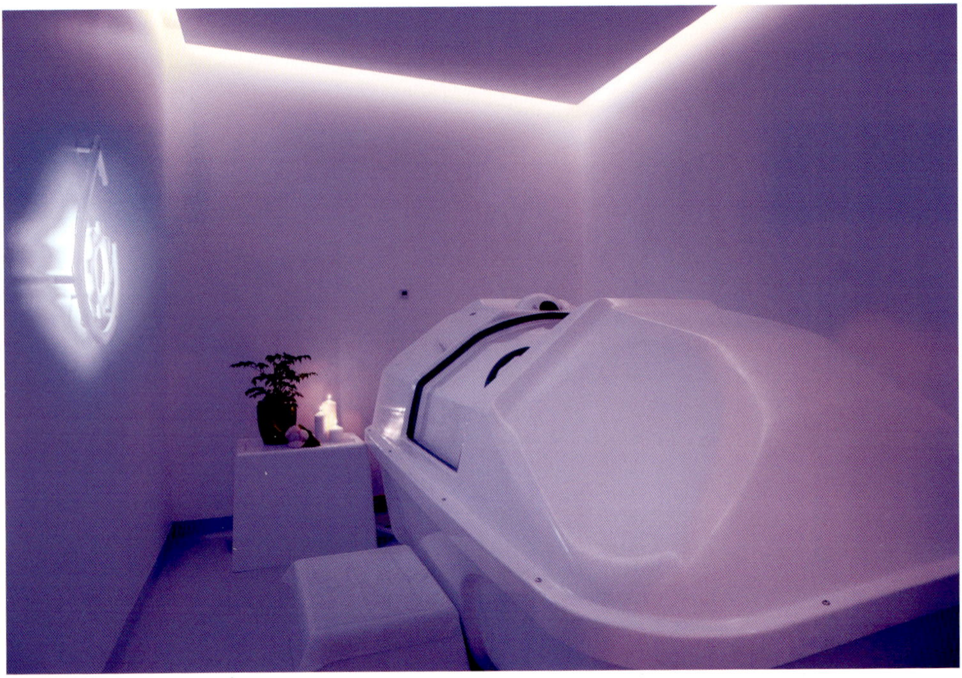

FLOAT FACTORY

131–145 Glebe Point Rd, Glebe

SERVICES /

Float Therapy

TAKE A WEIGHT OFF • Float Factory is a purpose-built floatation therapy centre, located in Glebe, with specially designed sensory deprivation tanks that allow you to experience complete weightlessness. As you float in more than 350kg of the highest-grade of Epsom salts, you'll feel zero sensory input to be able to shut off from the outside world in a safe and controlled environment. There are three private rooms available, all equipped with showers, ear plugs, towels and robes. With everything provided, there's nothing to bring but yourself and an open mind. Floating is a relaxing treatment that can help relieve stress and insomnia, increase focus and creativity and produce endorphins. Physically, a session can benefit sore muscles, increase blood flow and improve recovery by accelerating the removal of lactic acid.

FLOATFACTORY.COM.AU

SYDNEY FLOAT CENTRE

Brookvale & Darlinghurst

SERVICES /

Float Therapy

BEYOND THE BODY • Sydney Float Centre was created out of passion, enthusiasm and a belief in the benefits of floating to reduce stress and pain, and help people feel relaxed and rejuvenated. They offer the largest, finest and most advanced float tanks available, at two convenient locations in Sydney. The state-of-the-art centres in Darlinghurst and Brookvale are meticulously designed to create a calm and welcoming environment where you can stop in to unwind and rest, beyond mind and body. Their dedication to helping others is evident from the website, through to the phone, and the first time you walk in the door. You will know they love what they do and want you to feel welcome. So, take a chance and a moment for yourself, to unplug from your schedule and let your worries float away.

SYDNEYFLOATCENTRE.COM.AU

BY ADIE ROBERTSON / FOUNDER TO WONDERLAND

AN ANTIDOTE TO THE MODERN WORLD /

Stress is a contemporary endemic; a dangerous by-product of overstimulation, disconnection and fast-paced lifestyles. But there's a simple recipe to bring back balance – and it all starts inside.

IN MODERN SOCIETY, WE MULTI-TASK SO MUCH SO THAT WE'RE OPERATING IN A STATE OF CONSTANT OVERDRIVE.

From the moment we arise in the morning we're required to switch on our sympathetic nervous system - our stress response - add to that morning traffic, relationships, jobs, finances, etc and too often we continue to function in this state of 'fight or flight', our stresses are not necessarily resolved and we never actually relax. As a result, anger, frustration and intolerance are rife.

The parasympathetic nervous system simply does not get a chance to bring the body back to restorative mode. Our sympathetic nervous systems are running on overdrive to the point of burnout.

In stressful situations you may have noticed your blood pressure rising, your heart pounding, your muscles tensing accompanied by shallow fast breathing. At this stage adrenalin and cortisol are pumping through your veins putting you on high alert whilst the body stops all non-essential processes.

Stress is a real physical reaction and the most dangerous toxin in our bodies. It plays havoc with our gut-health, digestive and immune systems, skin health and our emotional and mental wellbeing - the damage is cumulative. Stress is a killer, recognised as a major contributing factor in cancer and heart disease and is associated with addictive disorders and depression. It harms our relationships, distorts who we really are, detracting from our enjoyment of life.

I believe that yoga and meditation are the panacea for our modern lifestyle, an antidote to stress and anxiety and a positive benefit to mental health. It is a powerful, preventative, prescriptive medicine and the benefits are cumulative. The more you do the better you feel. It activates the relaxation response, calming the nervous system and optimising the functions of the body systems, restoring balance and replenishing energy.

A regular Dru Yoga practice creates flexibility, alignment, stillness and strength in day to day life, replacing 'dis'ease with ease in mind, body and soul. It creates radiant health by releasing endorphins, boosting energy, building muscles, strengthening the body and improving performance. It brings relaxation, body awareness, confidence and zest for life. The combination of breath with movement, positive affirmations and visualisations is a potent mix. When done regularly, witness the transformation as your heart opens to humanity and your life opens up to possibility.

I prefer to practice outside in nature and the fresh air, to marvel at the world around me; the blue sky, the green grass, the warmth of the sun, the breeze in my hair. It quickly grounds me and brings me back to my true state of being - awakening joy, contentment, trust and a deep feeling of peace and knowing. It amplifies my intuition and reminds me to be humble and appreciative of the present moment while connecting me to the divine and my radiant light within.

Meditation is simple and can be done anywhere, at any time. Learning to reflect our gaze inwardly can have amazing results. Explore the vastness within you; take yourself on a journey to the feeling of freedom. Meditation facilitates clarity, mindfulness, purpose and wisdom, and promotes a long list of health benefits. It will facilitate you becoming less reactive in stressful situations. Meditators live longer. Ultimately, we have everything we need inside ourselves - we too often look to external factors for our happiness and gratification.

Adopting 'mudras' helps to develop an inward focus and direct the body's energy flow. As you hold your fingers and hands in different positions you harness the ability to energise and transform your mind and emotions.

Chanting mantra empowers our thoughts and prayers with repetition and focus. It raises our vibration and aligns us to our higher self. It is said when we chant in Sanskrit we bring the power of manifestation. Spirituality leads us into another dimension and supports our existence in this one.

MEDITATION EXERCISE

Settle into a comfortable sitting position with your spine erect. Adopt the Jnana Mudra, connecting the thumb and index finger leaving the other fingers straight. This will help to reduce mental tension and promote memory and concentration. A gesture of giving or receiving depending on whether the palms are facing up on dow

I invite you to close your eyes. Your brain will naturally produce alpha waves that are associated with relaxation and inner calm. Breathe in. Breathe out. Deeply. Accept your physicality, are you comfortable. Accept your environment, allow the noise to fade to the background. Accept your thoughts. Let them come and go, don't pay them any attention. Notice your breath. Feel your lungs expand and deflate. Feel the coolness of the in-breath. Feel the warmth of the out-breath. Breathe in peace. Breathe out peace.

Draw your palms together into the praying hands mudra, with your thumbs resting against your sternum. Notice how your awareness shifts to your inner being and a deep sense of peace arises from your heart.

SILENTLY AFFIRM:

I am peace. Feel peace in every cell of your body. In every sense of your being.Rest here awhile. Learn to see the world through eyes of gratitude; cast your glance wide, open your perspective. Find joy in the simple things. The often elusive key to happiness already exists within.

We do have the power to modify our future life by bringing change to the present moment.

n my defense,
he moon
vas full
nd I
vas left
nsupervise

BY ADIE ROBERTSON / FOUNDER TO WONDERLAND

CREATURES OF HABIT /

The secret to longevity is to live well. By gradually adopting good habits, you will amplify a sense of structure in your day and a sense of achievement within your life.

DAILY PRACTICES TO ENHANCE YOUR WELLBEING.

Establishing rituals around your habits brings a specialness to what you do; a sacred invitation to begin. For instance lighting candles for a bath, or a single flame for meditation, setting the table, saying grace before a meal or bowing your head for prayer will signify an intention to begin.

In our modern world there's so much 'stuff' to deal with on a continual basis, so it's vital to schedule exclusive time to yourself each day. This will bring a sense of pleasure, peace and accomplishment to your life, while negating the dangerous and cumulative effects of stress.

While spontaneity is the spice of life, establishing healthy habits and patterns is the framework for success and satisfaction. They provide us with a sense of purpose and the repetition of a habit builds *shakti* or energy, bringing us a sense of fulfilment.

In a time-poor society, work-life balance is important and will ultimately provide you with more freedom and happiness. You have the power to change the way your life looks and feels. Break the cycle. **Start today.**

BREATHE CONSCIOUSLY

When we learn to control our breath we control our minds. Breathing brings life to our physicality so learn to breathe effectively. Close your eyes and withdraw from the world around you. Come home to yourself. Breathe in deeply, expand your lungs slowly, and exhale. Relax. With each inhalation, notice your breath nourishing your lungs and with each exhalation relax a little more deeply. Let go.

When possible go outside in nature and go bare feet on the earth. Smell the fresh air and be truly thankful for it. For breath is life.

MOVE YOUR BODY

One step at a time, move towards fitness. Exercise is addictive; the feel-good endorphins will have you coming back for more. Staying physically active is the most important ingredient to ageing well. That said there's no time to waste. Movement begins with a mindset.

QUIET MEDITATION

With a calm, clear mind, the debris of a cluttered, disorganised life falls away leaving behind what's important. A meditation practice encourages us to take time out, to pause, to get grounded, to find peace and to realise what really matters. When you close your eyes, delight in the vastness within yourself, explore, go deep, stay awhile. The more time spent in quiet contemplation, the more shall be revealed.

Visualisations and positive affirmations will make your meditation practice more potent. Keep a journal handy and give life to your thoughts in the moments after with the power of intention or sankulpa; journaling actually reduces stress promoting greater wellbeing. Create a vision for how you want your life to look. Get really clear on what you want. Make an action plan. Go for it. Chase your wildest dreams and that which sets your soul on fire.

EAT WELL AND HYDRATE

Become aware of the food you eat and drink and begin to question what you are putting into your mouth. We literally are what we eat. Knowing that every 28 days our cells turn over, would you choose to be made of delicious, vital, non-GMO organic fresh food or processed artificial products, loaded with additives and wrapped up in plastic? Drink plenty of water to flush toxins and inflammation from your body.

SLEEP ENOUGH

A good night's sleep is an essential part of our wellbeing. Positively impacting cellular repair, immunity and relaxation it does wonders for our mood, focus, productivity, creativity, mental and physical health and of course our beauty. Set a regular bedtime where possible, avoid screen time close to lights out, try reading a book instead and cuddle if you can. Sweet dreams.

PRACTICE GRATITUDE

Gratitude was often quoted by the ancient philosophers: As Marcus Aurelius said: "When you arise in the morning, think of what a precious privilege it is to be alive - to breathe, to think, to enjoy, to love." Recent studies suggest that grateful people are happier, healthier, better rested, more motivated to exercise and enjoy better relationships; that gratitude is actually good for our health.

Life is our greatest gift after all.

Cherish it.

TO WONDERLAND /

Adie Robertson is the founder of To Wonderland in North Bondi. Originally a country girl, she lived in Hong Kong and London in her early thirties, before settling in the Southern Highlands of NSW to raise her young family. There, she began challenging the ideals of prescription medicine and processed food. A confident woman in her fifties, Adie exemplifies how a fit, healthy lifestyle can turn back the clock.

TOWONDERLAND.COM.AU

FOUNDER / HUGO TAYLOR BLACK

I didn't always have the opportunities I have now. I grew up with a poor support network that lacked the leadership I craved as a child. I suffered from a social anxiety disorder and barely spoke a word until I was around eight years old.

Despite my slow and challenging start in this world, the one thing I did have was passion to forge my own path. I realised there was so much more to life than what I had been told, or what people around me told me life should look like. I just hadn't worked out what I wanted instead.

At 16, I left school to begin a career in hospitality as an apprentice chef. It was hard work, but it kept me out of trouble and allowed me to start building discipline and confidence I needed. I loved expressing myself through the art of gastronomy.

I started my first business 13 years ago at age 24. Hugo's Health Packs was a simple idea, a healthy snack delivery service. My customers were treated to a few pieces of fruit, a yogurt with muesli and a small selection of nuts. I would deliver my packs every morning to businesses around the Sydney CBD. It barely covered my rent, I had no business plan, there was no social media. I just took the leap to make my idea a reality; living by my creed of doing what I loved.

The business only lasted six months before I sold everything I owned and travelled the world on an adventure of self-discovery. I explored and lived in many amazing locations: Norway, New York, Aspen, France, Mexico, Scotland, England and many other places in between. Every destination an opportunity to soak up foreign influence and culture. Learning and adapting to different values, beliefs and traditions.

It was around this time that I became fascinated by the fast-paced, constantly evolving world of digital design. What was a part-time obsession quickly became my full-time profession. It didn't take me long to realise that both visual art and digital design share the power to engage and emotionally connect with people. My talents were sought by a variety of clients, but something wasn't quite right.

On my return to Sydney, I noticed how contemporary lifestyles were affecting people's health. I saw an opportunity to make a difference and became determined to draw on the lessons I'd learned from my own successes, failures and challenges. I decided to use my design and communication skills to support health and wellness professionals in their quest to help others live better, healthier and happier lives. That's when Empowered was born.

Empowered is an online digital marketing agency and we're passionate about crafting website and SEO strategies for health and wellness businesses. We work with all types of wellness professionals, such as personal trainers, gyms, yoga centres, Pilates studios, spas and wellness centres. Basically, we support anyone who is in the business of changing people's lives.

Through my work with these incredible businesses, I became inspired. So many people are doing amazing things for the health of their communities and it has become my mission to showcase them.

The Wellness Guide embodies this passion for helping people and connecting communities. It is a reflection of who I am and who I want to be.

I've poured my heart and soul into this book. I hope you enjoy it as much as I've enjoyed creating it.

HUGO TAYLOR BLACK

Founder The Wellness Guide

A-Z LOCATION INDEX /

A-Z LOCATION INDEX /

A-Z LOCATION INDEX /

A-Z LOCATION INDEX /

THE WELLNESS GUIDE / SYDNEY EDITION

thewellnessguide.com.au

Created by Hugo Taylor Black

WITH THANKS TO THE FOLLOWING FOR THEIR CONTRIBUTIONS:

Adie Robertson, Falsegrip, Fitness Playground, Jackie Alexander, Jessica Sepel, Jonnie Pollard, Josh Porteous, Keiran Barry, Libby Babet, Mark Brewer, Melissa Ambrosini and Scott Gooding.

PHOTOGRAPHY BY:

Provided by Venues, Amy Fraser, Andrew Worssam, Dominic Loneragan, Edward De Simone, Hellene Algie, Honeydieu Fitography Hugo Taylor Black, Joel Pratley, Katherine Lu, Natalia Horinkova and Romy Frydman.

Includes Index

ISBN 978-0-646-59853-6

For PR, marketing and stockist opportunities, contact editorsyd@thewellnessguide.com.au